Color
for
Quilters II

◆

Susan
McKelvey

©1993 by Susan Richardson McKelvey

Photographs by the Holmes I. Metee Studio, Inc., Baltimore, MD, 1983

Cover quilt, *Sunset Flight* by Susan McKelvey, 1982.

Design and production coordination by Gillian Johnson,
Illustration and Art Direction by Cynthia Edmiston,
Merrifield Graphics & Publishing Service, Inc., Hanover, Maryland

Published by Wallflower Designs
1161 Goldfinch Lane
Millersville, MD 21108

ISBN 0-9639963-0-4

Library of Congress Cataloging-in-Publication Data

McKelvey, Susan Richardson.
Color for quilters II/ by Susan McKelvey
Includes bibliographical references
ISBN 0-9639963-0-4

Printed in Hong Kong by Regent Publishing Services, Ltd.
First Edition

9 8 7 6 5 4 3 2 1

◆ Dedication ◆

To Doug, Leslie and Scott McKelvey,
who color my life with love

◆ Acknowledgments ◆

There are many people without whose help I could not have written *Color for Quilters II*. First, I must thank again the many people who helped me collect, make, and quilt the samples in 1982: my friends in the New Image Quilters, whose quilts so beautifully illustrate color theory: Caryl Rae Hancock, Kathy Kolsevich, Dominie Nash, Nancy Nelson, and Sue Pierce; Ellen Swanson, whose antique quilts illustrate so well how universal color theory is; and my friends from The Annapolis Quilt Guild, who lent quilts and helped quilt samples: Mary Sharp, Teresa Duley, Jackie Janovsky, Rose Beach, Patricia Curtis, Mary Dattore, Metta Lansdale, Shirley McFadden, Anna Marie McFadden, Rhoda Miller, Susan Miller, Lori Roth, and Ann Warner. In addition, my thanks go to my book designer, Gillian Johnson, and Cynthia Edmiston of Merrifield Graphics & Publishing Service, Inc., and to Marsha McCloskey and Ami Simms for their help and encouragement.

◆ Contents ◆

◆ A Colorful Journey ◆

"If you, unknowing, are able to create masterpieces in color,
then unknowledge is your way. But if you are unable to
create masterpieces in color out of your unknowledge,
then you ought to look for knowledge."

Johannes Itten[1]

It is a pleasure to be printing a revised and greatly improved edition of *Color for Quilters*, published originally in 1984. It was the first book on color written especially for quilters, by a quilter, and using quilts as examples.

Much has been written in the years since 1984 about color, and the quilting world is richer for the great variety of information. But *Color for Quilters*, with simple language and clear projects, remains the quintessential basic text. I hope it will help many of you to continue the quest we started together over a decade ago and will encourage those of you who are eager to conquer color to join us as we accept the challenge of color.

I began my research into color out of frustration. I was making lovely but unpredictable quilts, and I didn't understand why I often got effects different from what I had planned. Even though I designed before sewing, things happened in the piecing that I couldn't predict, and I couldn't solve problems I had created by accident. When I asked quilt teachers, they didn't know the answers or told me to "use my intuition." I **had** been using my intuition, but too often that wasn't enough. So I began to study color theory on my own. And the things I found out were marvelous! The information I gleaned actually helped me solve my design problems.

This precious information on how color affects design was not then, and is not now, secret information. It is the stuff of which art education is made. It is the theory in which art students immerse themselves throughout the long years of their art training. And, as they repeatedly experiment with color theory, it **does** become intuitive. To those who bring their art background to quilting, color theory is intuitive. But to many of us for whom art training ended in high school, it is not. To tell a beginning quilter who has had no art training to "use your intuition" leaves the beginner with nowhere to turn.

Color for Quilters II, then, is for those of you who have felt that you have nowhere to turn. It brings color theory down to the reality of fabric and thread and gives practical aid to beginners. You don't necessarily want to become an expert in color theory, but you do want to be able to solve problems when they arise in designing. Learning some basic color terms and concepts will enable you to design beautiful quilts.

CHAPTER 1

◆ Color Comes First ◆

Color in quilts, as in all art, is what strikes the viewer first. It is the impact of a quilt's color that attracts or repels us, that leads us to examine other elements of the quilt. The stitching may be exquisite and the piecing flawless, but unless the colors are compelling, the quilt fails to command our attention.

Color, then, is the **grabber**, the **eye-catcher**, the **lure**. It is not the specific color that matters—a red quilt may catch your eye despite the fact that red is not your favorite color. It is the **play** of color that catches the eye. Once you are caught, you may savor any number of a quilt's qualities—workmanship, number of stitches per inch, complexity of piecing, mitered corners, or originality of design. But these are close-up judgements. **Color comes first!**

Since the use of color can make or break a quilt, it is not enough to "trust your own intuition" or "use your favorite colors"—at least not once you are beyond your first quilt. Serious quilters enjoy treating color seriously.

Color theory applies to quilts. The quilts we love are memorable precisely because, consciously or unconsciously, their makers used valid color principles. You, too, can use these principles. They are logical and understandable. There are terms you must learn, but they are presented here in logical order with simple explanations. By the time you have read and worked through the projects in **The Workbook**, you, too, will be prepared to meet the color challenge.

8

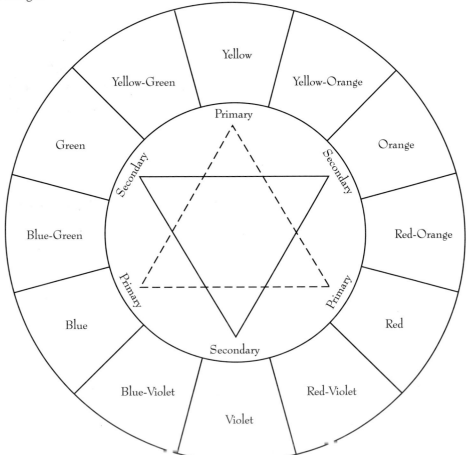

CHAPTER 2

◆ The Color Wheel ◆

It is necessary to begin with some terms, a vocabulary with which to discuss color. Let's start with the basic structure of color—the color wheel. The wheel opposite and the colored version on page 34 is a twelve color wheel. It is the most familiar wheel and gives us the information we need to discuss color.[2] As we discuss the terms, refer to them.

Primary Colors

Many of you will remember from elementary school art classes that there are three *primary* colors: red, yellow, and blue. These are called *primary* because it is from these three that all other colors are mixed. Notice on the wheel that these are positioned at the three points of an equilateral triangle.

Secondary Colors

There are three *secondary* colors: orange, green, and purple. They are the second set of colors and are simple combinations of the primary colors:

red	+	yellow	=	orange
yellow	+	blue	=	green
blue	+	red	=	purple

Tertiary Colors

The colors made by combining primary and secondary colors are *tertiary* colors, or the third set of colors. Mix blue and green to get blue-green, green and yellow to get yellow-green, continuing around the wheel. The term *tertiary* isn't as important as are the colors and their positions on the wheel.

The Entire Color Wheel

Using this color wheel and knowing its twelve colors will enable us to discuss color vocabulary.

Chapter 3

◆ Color Terms ◆

Colors or Hues

Hue is another word for *color*. The color wheel contains twelve distinct colors, each one different from the others. We may talk about the many hues in a quilt or the many colors. I use the word *color* throughout this book.

Pure Colors

The colors on our wheel are all of the same *intensity*. They are clear, strong, and rich: the reddest red and the bluest blue possible. They are what we call *pure* colors, with no other colors added. We can change these pure colors in two ways: in *value* and in *intensity*.

Value

We may take any one of the pure colors and make it darker or lighter (as if in mixing paints, we added black or white). If we make it darker, it is called a *shade*. If we make it lighter, it is called a *tint*.

10   *Shade* is a term we already know and use frequently. If someone says she used several shades of blue in her quilt, we know immediately what she means. She may have used navy, royal blue, and baby blue and is calling them shades of blue. If she were using color terms more precisely, she would say she used three *values* of blue—a shade, a pure blue, and a tint. But whichever she says, quilters understand that she made a blue quilt, containing three values.

Value, then, is a concept with which we are all familiar, even thought the term may be new. There may be many gradations of value from black to white. Look at Figure 6 on page 47, which shows a pure blue centered between shades on the left and tints on the right. Look also at the color wheel quilt on page 35. This is my lecture quilt, made in 1983 from fabrics available at the time, so the colors do not perfectly match the pure colors of the true color wheel. But that doesn't matter. Any color wheel gives us the basis for discussion, and thus it is more important that we know where red lies on the wheel than that the red fabric be a perfect red.

Notice that on this quilt, there are three circles. The middle circle is the basic color wheel, made up of the pure colors. The inner circle contains tints of each pure color, while the outer circle contains shades. Thus, you see three values of each color. We could also show many values of each pure color on the wheel or in a design.

Intensity

The colors on the twelve color wheel are pure colors. To say it another way, they are the most intense versions of themselves; they are strong. We may take any one of the pure colors and make it grayer or duller, thus changing its intensity and making it weaker. As we add gray to any color, the color loses its intensity and vibrance. It then becomes a *tone of* its pure color. The pure colors on the color wheel have no gray in them— they have the greatest intensity or purity of color. A *tone* is a grayed version of a pure color. Think of the phrase "to tone down"; that's what we do when we gray a color. Look at Figure 7 on page 47, which shows a pure blue from the color wheel centered between two dark grayed and two light grayed blues.

Chroma

Chroma is the Greek root meaning *color*. It is a useful term because it allows us to use the words below, which are derived from it.

Achromatic

We may refer to quilts as *achromatic*. *A* means *without,* so an achromatic quilt is one without color or a quilt made of the non-colors: black, white, gray, or any combination.

Monochromatic

Monochromatic means one color, and this, too, is a useful term for quilters. It describes a quilt made entirely in one color, although it may contain many values of that color. A monochromatic color scheme is a popular combination in quilting and one of the most successful because it is easy to do. It is a *safe* color scheme because it almost always works. It is, therefore, a good one for beginners. Look at *February Blues* on page 44, a monochromatic quilt in only one color—blue. But it has life and texture because the maker used many values of blue and many fabrics of different prints.

11

Polychromatic

Polychromatic means many-colored, and although we don't use this word frequently, we use the concept often—every time we make a multi-colored quilt. Look at *Mariner's Lily* and *Amish Baskets* on pages 40 and 41. Within each are many colors, making them good examples of polychromatic quilts.

Analogous

Analogous colors are ones right next to each other on the color wheel. Many exciting quilts are based on combinations of analogous colors. Analogous color schemes work well because the colors are so closely related. You can't go wrong combining them. Look at *Evening Star* on page 44. Although there are many fabrics in the quilt, they are all values of only blue and purple, two analogous colors. The variety of fabrics and values provides interest, but the color scheme is a simple analogous one.

A Block Changes

On page 36 are three different versions of one quilt block, *Joseph's Coat*. They are excellent examples of the color terms we have discussed. Let's analyze their color schemes.

Block A uses an achromatic color scheme. It has no color, only several values of black, gray and white. What keeps it from being boring is variety in value and fabrics, making it an interesting block despite its lack of color.

Block B uses a monochromatic color scheme. It is made of only one color, blue, but relies on variety in value and prints to avoid dullness.

Block C uses a polychromatic and analogous color scheme. It is made of two colors, blue and purple, which are next to each other on the color wheel, but it includes a variety of both values and prints.

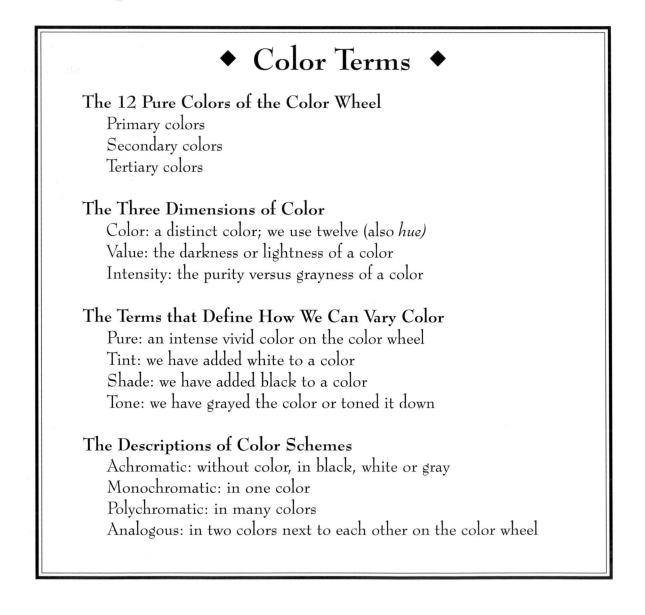

◆ Color Terms ◆

The 12 Pure Colors of the Color Wheel
Primary colors
Secondary colors
Tertiary colors

The Three Dimensions of Color
Color: a distinct color; we use twelve (also *hue)*
Value: the darkness or lightness of a color
Intensity: the purity versus grayness of a color

The Terms that Define How We Can Vary Color
Pure: an intense vivid color on the color wheel
Tint: we have added white to a color
Shade: we have added black to a color
Tone: we have grayed the color or toned it down

The Descriptions of Color Schemes
Achromatic: without color, in black, white or gray
Monochromatic: in one color
Polychromatic: in many colors
Analogous: in two colors next to each other on the color wheel

CHAPTER 4

◆ Apply the Color Terms to Quilts ◆

Before we continue our exploration of color, let's look at a few of the quilts in the book, keeping the color terms in mind.

Quilts Which Vary Value and Tone

Most quilts play with value and/or tone in some way. For example, let's look at several pieces which only play with these two color factors. *Matter of Choice* on page 41 plays with several values of red. *Evening Star* on page 44 uses many values of the two analogous colors, blue and purple. *Plaids*, the pair of blocks in Figure 8 on page 47, plays with color intensity. The pure colors are in the centers of the blocks, and fabrics become grayer as they go outward to the edges.

Monochromatic Quilts

The *Plaids* blocks are also monochromatic. *February Blues* on page 44 is a vibrant example of playing with many values of one color. *Homespun Revisited*, page 42, also relies mostly on value for its variety.

Polychromatic Quilts

Many quilts are polychromatic. As examples, look at these quilts: *Colors of My Day* on page 33, *Double Irish Chain* on page 39, *Amish Baskets* on page 41, and *Mariner's Lily* on page 40. Notice also that the pair of quilts on page 45, *Six on Black* and *Six on White,* use only the six pure primary and secondary colors.

Summary

Thus, you can see that the terms we have discussed in Chapter 3 apply to quilts. They are important terms to know, not for themselves, but because they are the tools we will use to learn how colors work and how we can make them work **for** us rather than **against** us. Before we continue, stop and take a survey of your own quilts and those of your friends, using these color terms.

13

TIME OUT TO EXPERIMENT

This book is based on the premise that you will try each color principle, putting it into your own terms of fabric and color. So at the end of each section, I send you to **The Workbook** at the back of the book. Take your time doing each project and examining it later to see what you accomplished. Although all the projects are designed to be done quickly in pasteup form, they should provide you with jumping off places for actual quilts, too. Turn to **The Workbook**. Read the introduction; then do Worksheets 1 - 3 to help you understand the color terms.

CHAPTER 5

◆ Harmony ◆

Your goal in making a quilt (aside from warmth, of course) is to make a **pleasing** quilt. Just as in decorating a room or coordinating a wardrobe, your goal is harmony. You want colors to go together, to balance. One color may dominate, but no color should clash or destroy the harmony. This definition of *harmony* assumes it is a purely subjective idea.

Personal Taste (Subjective Harmony)

If we ask each person in a group of quilters to choose a set of harmonious colors, each set will be different. This is *subjective* harmony, dictated by individual preference and taste. This is one harmony we discuss and strive for throughout this book.

But color theory goes beyond the idea of **what** colors a person likes to explain **why** a person likes them and to include color principles that can be proved objectively. We want to become aware of how these color principles can help us make harmonious quilts.

Gray Equals Equilibrium

Scientists have shown that the human eye **needs** a state of equilibrium. Color theorists agree that the state of color equilibrium is a neutral gray.[3]

Harmony thus can be achieved when the colors we use would make gray if they were mixed together. For example, black and white mixed make gray. Certain colors mixed together equal gray, too, and are thus harmonious. This leads us to additional color terms.

Complements

For every color on the wheel, there is a *complement*. It is the color directly opposite that color on the wheel. Look at the color wheel on page 34. Notice that the complement of yellow is purple, of red is green, and of blue is orange. To complement something means *to finish it* (not compliment, now; that is what we hope to receive when we have finished our quilts!). In our eyes' striving for harmony or balance, that is exactly what this opposite color does—it finishes the color. If they were paints mixed together, the two complements would make gray. All pairs of complements on the wheel go to gray as they mix.

Possibly you remember experiments as children where you stared at a color for 30 seconds, then closed your eyes and saw a different color? The color you see is the complement. Try it again, if you want. Stare at something red on a white background for 30 seconds or more. Then cover the dot with white. You will see a green afterimage. This happens because the human eye automatically provides the complement to achieve balance and harmony, and, thus, all complementary pairs of colors are harmonious.

Other Harmonious Color Combinations

Other combinations of colors can be harmonious, too. We discussed how analogous color combinations are harmonious because the colors are closely related on the color wheel. Other harmonious combinations can be found by superimposing different figures on our color wheel and turning them. If we impose an equilateral triangle, the colors at the three points of that triangle are harmonious, no matter where you position the triangle, and artists call this triadic harmony.

The colors on the corners of an isosceles triangle are also harmonious. So are the colors on the four corners of a square or rectangle.[4] Turning these figures in different ways gives us new ideas about harmonious color combinations—ideas we may not have considered before. These are the four shapes used to find harmonious combinations of color:

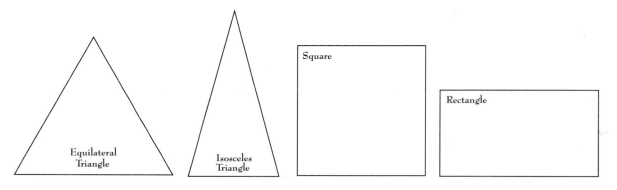

Equilateral Triangle

Isosceles Triangle

Square

Rectangle

I have provided patterns for them on Worksheet 5 for your use in experimenting on Worksheet 6. Fabric designers and artists in all fields use these triangles and tetrads to find new and unusual color combinations. The combinations which develop through the use of these shapes are often ones you wouldn't think of without a formula. That is why mind-stretching exercises which force you to play with new harmonies are useful.

Objective Harmony

Thus, we see that we can use objective guidelines to help us in choosing harmonious color combinations. These guidelines are not meant to limit us but to lead us to discover color combinations new to us. We all are limited by our experience and preferences and can benefit from new ideas on color. Yet, even after learning about objective color harmony, we will still return to our **personal** color ideas in our work. And that is all right.

TIME OUT TO EXPERIMENT
Do Worksheets 4 - 6 to help you understand complements and color harmony.

Chapter 6

◆ Contrast ◆

Contrast is the use of two different things together. There are several different kinds of color contrast. We will discuss seven:

1. color contrast
2. complementary contrast
3. contrast of value
4. warm-cool contrast[5]
5. contrast of color strength
6. contrast in intensity
7. simlutaneous contrast

Don't let this list intimidate you. We use these kinds of contrast all the time, but we don't break them down and discuss them in this way. We will examine them one at a time, giving examples as we go and following each contrast with experiments in **The Workbook**.

Color Contrast

Color contrast simply means the contrast we get when we put together two or more different colors. Any quilt in several colors is polychromatic and uses contrast of color. We do this all the time!

The strongest color contrast is between the strongest colors—the twelve pure colors on the color wheel. Using any of these pure colors together will create a vibrant quilt. We are familiar with the use of the three primary colors together in children's items. When we combine them, we get strong color contrast because we are using pure colors.

Traditional folk art often relies on strong color contrast. Pennsylvania Dutch designs combine the primary colors in their designs. Mexican folk art uses the bright colors of the color wheel. Stained glass relies on color contrast for its effects.

Complementary Contrast

Complementary contrast is the use of any two complements together.

Complements Used Equally Vibrate

Placing two complements right next to each other produces the strongest complementary contrast. In fact, if you put two complements next to each other and in equal proportions, they vibrate so much that they are frequently hard to look at and can be overwhelming. The antique red and green *Mill Wheel* on page 38 uses the complements equally, and is, thus, a vibrating quilt despite years of fading.

Complements Used Unequally Add Spark and Accent

Used unequally, however, one complement becomes the accent, the spark that gives the quilt life. Thus, the trick to using complements together is to use them unequally.

Peony Medallion on page 39 uses red and green unequally. The red dominates, and the dark green supports it, while the white background dilutes the strong contrast of complements together. The green is, thus, the accent color. *Compromise* on page 37 uses navy and rust (two dark values of blue and orange) together unequally. These quilts are good examples of the use of two complementary colors in unequal proportions.

In Chapter 3, we discussed the monochromatic color scheme. It is safe, pleasing, and usually works well. Sometimes, however, it can be dull. This is partly because, as we learned in Chapter 5, the eye physically demands the complement of a color for harmony. Because the eye needs the complement, the complement often makes the perfect accent color for a quilt.

How to Add a Complementary Accent

We may add a touch of the complement by using a fabric in the complementary color or by finding a print which contains complementary contrast within it. The three *Mexican Cross* blocks on page 37 illustrate two ways to add the complement. Block A is a monochromatic block—all blues. In Block B, I substituted a navy fabric with tiny rust flowers for the navy with white in Block A. In Block C, I wanted to add the complement, which is orange. I added a rust fabric (a dark value of orange) in the center squares to give a touch of the complement. Thus, Blocks B and C each contain a touch of the complement of the main color, but the effect is achieved in different ways.

All Values of a Complement are Complementary

Notice in the *Mexican Cross* blocks that we can use any value of the complements and achieve the same effect. Rust and peach are simply different values of orange; navy and light blue are simply different values of blue. They are all complementary, and a quilt benefits from a variety of values in its complementary contrast.

Knowing the complements of colors is a great help to quilters. Haven't you ever stared at a quilt that is dull or unsuccessful and tried to figure out what it needs, what's missing? Perhaps what's missing is the **spark** of a complementary color. Take the time to learn and to play with complementary pairs of colors. It will be time well spent.

TIME OUT TO EXPERIMENT
Do Worksheet 7 to help you understand the concept of complementary contrast.

Contrast of Value

Contrast of value or light-dark contrast is a color concept with which we quilters are familiar. We have been using it for generations. Such traditional quilt blocks as the *Log Cabin* **depend** on this contrast of light and dark to be successful, and quilt names such as *Sunshine and Shadow* are based on it.

Light & Dark Values Next to Each Other

The strongest light-dark contrast is achieved when we put very light and very dark values right next to each other. This makes powerful contrast.

Medium Values Dilute Light-Dark Contrast

When we put medium values between the light and dark fabrics, we dilute the strong light-dark contrast. We can dilute it by using a large range of values or just a few. Gray, a medium value of the ultimate light-dark contrast (black and white) acts in the same way to dilute light-dark contrast.

    Before continuing, take a moment to look at some quilts which use light-dark contrast. First, the three *Joseph's Coat* blocks on page 36 we examined before rely on contrast of value to create most of their interest. In Blocks A and B, there is no color contrast, so only the play of lights and darks makes the blocks interesting. Any quilt with very little color contrast (any monochromatic piece) needs some contrast, and, therefore, usually relies on contrast of value. Return to *Matter of Choice* (p. 41), and *February Blues* and *Evening Star* (both on p. 44). Contrast of value plays an important part in the designs of each of these quilts. *Compromise* on page 37 is a strong quilt in complementary contrast, but it would be a very dark quilt without the spark of white diamonds and border. It needed light-dark contrast in addition to its complementary contrast.

◆ **TIME OUT TO EXPERIMENT**
Do Worksheet 8 to help you understand contrast of value.

Warm-Cool Contrast

The warmth or coolness of the colors you use in a quilt affects every aspect of color contrast. It affects color contrast, light-dark contrast, and complementary contrast. Therefore, it is an important aspect of color selection.

Colors Have Temperature

Scientists have proved that colors have temperature and that this temperature affects people's moods. This is not true physical temperature, but lies in color's aesthetic qualities.[6] Cool colors are the blues and greens of the sky and the sea. Warm colors are the reds, oranges, and yellows of fire and the sun. On the color wheel, you see that yellow is at the top and purple is at the bottom. The cool colors are on the left; the warm colors are on the right.

Johannes Itten describes an experiment in a factory in which one workroom was painted blue-green, another red-orange. The occupants felt a temperature difference of five to seven degrees![7]

He describes a similar experiment with a horse stable. Half of the stable was painted blue, the other half red-orange. In the blue section, horses soon quieted down after running, but in the red section, they remained hot and restless for some time. It was found that there were no flies in the blue section, and a great many in the red section.[8] Even animals seem to be affected by the psychology of color temperature.

Cool Soothes But Warm Stimulates

So use the cool blues and greens when you want a soothing quilt or a calming effect (or don't want to attract flies!). *Evening Star* on page 44 is a wonderful example of a cool quilt in blues, grays, and lavenders, as is *February Blues* below it.

Hospitals, schools, advertisers, restaurants, businesses—all use the warm-cool principle to affect our behavior. For example, since "soft, warm colors . . .make food more palatable,"[9] fine restaurants often use soft peach and rose in their decor. But notice the word *soft*; colors must be soft tints or grayed tones of the pure warm colors to keep from being more stimulating than restful. Since red is an exciting color, "some football teams meet in a red room before the game. To calm them down and provide some rest, the team goes into a blue room during the half time period."[10]

Look at *Lady of the Lake* (p. 38) with its bright red lattice and *Double Irish Chain* (p. 39), dominated by pure yellow and red for two examples of stimulating quilts.

We, too, can use warm and cool colors to stimulate or sooth. It's simply a matter of planning. Use the cool colors of blue and green when you want to sooth or calm and the warm reds, oranges, and yellows when you want a strong, stimulating, exciting quilt.

Cool Recedes But Warm Advances

The fact that cool and warm colors behave differently when they are used together is the single most important color concept we need to understand. Cool colors recede or fade into the background. Warm colors advance or come forward. A cool color will become the background whether you intended it or not. Put blue stars on a red background, and you will have an entirely different quilt—red squares on a blue, starry background.

Notice which color advances in *Amish Baskets* on page 41. We usually think of the pieced blocks in a quilt as being the main design and of the connecting blocks as being the background. But in this quilt, the connecting blocks are equally strong because of their color. They are made of a warm, pure magenta right off the color wheel. Because the other colors are also strong, the whole quilt is a powerful example of color contrast, but there is no doubt which part of the quilt the viewer sees first.

Look again at the antique *Lady of the Lake* on page 38. Here again color changes the design. The pieced blocks are not the main element of the quilt. The lattice strips (usually not designed to dominate) catch the eye of the viewer first because of color. The pieced blocks are made of mostly cool blues, grays, and pale colors, while the lattice is made of bright red. So what we see first is the grid of the lattice, while the diagonal pattern of the pieced blocks seems to be in back of a red window frame.

This is why it is so important to understand warm-cool contrast. It is the color principle that affects a quilt more than any other and which you should consider in the planning stage, not after piecing.

Designing on graph paper or with a computer graphics program, using colored pencils, or pasting-up fabric will help you visualize which area of the quilt you want to advance. Use warm colors there. Use cool colors in areas you want to recede.

Warmth & Coolness Apply to All Values & Tones

The concept of the warmth and coolness of colors applies to all values of all colors. In a quilt made in pinks and blues of equal value, the pink will dominate because it is the warmer color. In a quilt made entirely of soft grayed colors, the warm colors will dominate. This is why you must consider color choices early in your quiltmaking.

Color Warmth is Relative

When we refer to a color as warm or cool, it has this character **in relation** to other colors we are using with it. Look at the two *Fan* blocks in Figure 9 on page 47. Color A is the same in both blocks. But its warmth is relative to the colors used with it. When used with red and orange, it is the coolest color. But the same fabric used with blue and turquoise becomes the warmest color. So, although the colors on the color wheel each have a warm or cool charac-ter, when we pick several specific fabrics for a quilt, we have a less clear set of colors.

The best way to practice seeing the relative warmth of colors is to play with bolts of fabric in a store or pieces from your collection. Stack the bolts of fabric on a table and step back from them at least five feet or spread out the fabrics. If you are fortunate enough to be near-sighted or astigmatic, take off your glasses, and you will see only the blur of color (I speak from experience!). One fabric will jump out at you. This is the dominant color. Using the color terms we have discussed, see if you can figure out why that color dominates. Is it purer? Is it warm? Then change the colors in your set to see what color dominates.

Harder to do but just as important is to assess the relative warmth of similar colors. Beiges are good examples. Beiges have a cast from rosy to greenish. Collect a set of beige fabrics and try to see which are warmer or cooler in feeling. This is difficult to do but worth practicing to show yourself that even colors of low intensity are affected by the warmth factor.

Warm & Cool Colors Together are Exciting

Using warm and cool colors together creates movement and vibration. The resulting quilt is strong and lively. Look again at *Amish Baskets* on page *41*. It virtually vibrates with color. So does *Mariner's Lily* on page *40*. Both rely almost entirely on warm-cool contrast and use mostly pure colors right off the color wheel. The combination of pure color and high warm-cool contrast is what makes the quilts so vibrant. If you want an exciting quilt, combine the warm and cool colors, and let them work for you.

Always be aware of the relative warmth of your colors. A bit of a warm color in a cool quilt can have the same enlivening effect as a bit of the complement. In fact, if you look at the color wheel, you will see that the complement of a color is always on the opposite side of the temperature scale. So, when you put in a bit of the complement, you are tossing in a bit of warm-cool contrast, too.

TIME OUT TO EXPERIMENT
Do Worksheets 9 and 10 to help you understand the concept of warm-cool contrast.

Contrast of Color Strength

The term *contrast of color strength* may seem unfamiliar and threatening. It's not! Simply stated, it recognizes that different colors have different strengths and, therefore, must be used in different proportions if you want to achieve harmony. When designing a quilt, you must consider the personalities or strengths of the colors you want to use in order to achieve balance.

Yellow is Strongest

Colors have different strengths and different brilliance. Let's use the pure colors of the color wheel for our discussion. Yellow is the most brilliant color of all and, thus, the strongest. Therefore, when planning a quilt, we need much less yellow in proportion to other colors. Look at *Double Irish Chain* on page 39. Notice how the yellow hits you first. Even on the color wheel, yellow jumps out at you. You need very little yellow in a quilt to achieve a powerful effect.

Harmonious Proportions of Colors

Figure 1 on page 46 shows harmonious proportions of complementary colors.[11] If you want to make a quilt that appears to have equal amounts of two complements, you actually use the colors unequally. You can see that if you choose to make a yellow and purple quilt, you need much less yellow than purple for the illusion of equality. You need much less orange than blue. But red and green are equal in strength (which is why used equally they vibrate). We discussed balance and harmony; this chart of proportion helps you estimate how to achieve that harmony. *Six on Black* and *Six on White* (p. 45) are a pair of quilts made to experiment with these proportions. They contain the six primary and secondary colors in proportion and in the same placement, varying only the background color (see discussion on page 25). Notice which colors catch the eye. Look again at *Mariner's Compass* on page 40. In it, the warm red and orange lily, despite being in tiny proportion to the cool blues and purples of the rest of the quilt, is what immediately catches the eye.

Warm Colors are Stronger than Cool

The color wheel in Figure 2 on page 46 has been altered to show the colors in *harmonious proportions* according to their strengths.[12] Notice that a little yellow goes a long way. In fact,

21

a little of all the warm colors goes a long way. In each pair of complements, the warm colors are in smaller proportion relative to the cool colors. This is because of their color strength. Being aware of color strength before putting our quilts together can help us control strong colors and make them work for us rather than against us.

Look again at *Compromise* on page 37. This is really a two-color quilt in complementary contrast. But because the rust is stronger than the blue and used in larger quantity, the quilt is dominated by the rust, while the blue recedes into the background. *Lady of the Lake* (p. 38) also shows how color strength can control a quilt. Although the red is used in small proportion to the overall dimension of the quilt, it dominates because of its color strength.

Generally speaking, the stronger the color, the less you use of it. If you have a large area to fill, use a weaker color.

◆ **TIME OUT TO EXPERIMENT**
Do Worksheet 11 to help you understand the concept of color strength.

Contrast of Intensity

When we refer to the intensity of a color, we mean the degree of purity or grayness of a color. Contrast of intensity is the contrast between pure, intense colors and dull, grayed colors.[13] Using a pure color with its duller tones makes a lovely design. Traditional plaids and woven designs are often based on this theme. The mix of pure and toned down color is contrast of intensity and is illustrated in the pair of *Plaids* blocks (Figure 8, page 47) in cool blues and warm pinks. In both blocks, the pure color is placed in the center, with grayed versions of that color from dark to light going out toward the edge.

When colors of different intensity are used together, the purest will dominate. The pure colors of the color wheel are, by definition, the most brilliant and intense, and this makes them strong when mixed with toned down or grayed colors.

Simultaneous Contrast

Our final contrast is called simultaneous contrast. It refers to how colors influence each other when we put them next to each other. Put the same gray against first a black background and then a white background, and it looks like two different grays—lighter on black and darker on white.

Put the same gray on a colored background and it takes on tinges of the color's complement.[14]

Simultaneous contrast works with two colors together as well as with gray and colors. The larger area influences the smaller. If we put two complements together, the larger area makes the smaller look more intense. So, if we want an accent to appear sharper, we can put it right next to its complement.

But there are times when we might want to avoid simultaneous contrast. If we want intricate small differences within a pattern to show, we avoid using a strong complement as background so the background doesn't detract from the subtle things happening within the design.

TIME OUT TO EXPERIMENT
Do Worksheet 12 to help you understand contrast of intensity and simultaneous contrast.

Uh Oh! All Kinds of Contrast at Once

We have now discussed seven kinds of color contrast. All of them can be found in quilts and can be used in designing.

It is important to remember that there are always several types of contrast at work at any time. For example, if you use the complements blue and orange, you are also putting warm-cool contrast into play. It helps to remember that the strengths of these two colors are different and use them proportionately.

If you use the complements yellow and purple together, you are immediately adding light-dark contrast, and, because yellow is the strongest of all colors, proportion plays a major role in your planning.

We usually **want** multiple contrasts. They give a quilt life. Strong contrast of any kind will emphasize lines and contours. But, sometimes there may be too much going on. If so, stand back to look at the quilt and analyze what and how many types of contrasts have been incorporated.

When you plan a quilt, and when you're playing with fabric, be aware of contrast. If the quilt seems too dull, what kind of contrast can you add? If it is too wild, with too much happening, what kind of contrast can you remove or quiet down? Perhaps there is contrast of hue, of value, and of warmth all at once, and it's too strong. Subduing just one of these might simplify the quilt. Try different approaches to quiet or enliven a quilt.

Which Colors Dominate?

A dominant color is one that takes over the quilt or becomes the main focus. In our discussion of color contrast, we discussed the many factors that contribute to which color dominates at any time in a design. If many kinds of contrast are going on in a quilt at the same time, different things happen. But, in general, we can rely on several principles:

These Colors Dominate	These Colors Recede
Pure or intense colors	Grayed or pale colors
Warm colors	Cool colors
Dark values	Light values

23

The question of whether dark or light values dominate is complicated by many other factors. How much of a color is used affects which appears stonger. Sometimes a dark color becomes shadow and thus recedes, but for the most part, when you look at a design to anaylyze which parts stand out and why, you will find that the dark areas, provided they are not fighting for dominance with pure and warm colors, will attract your eyes.

Starry Variation on page 36 is an experimental quilt which grew out of the three blocks above it. These three *Joseph's Coat* blocks were made for this book to illustrate achromatic, monochromatic, and analogous color schemes, as we have discussed. But in comparing the blocks, I noticed that the design changed each time I made a new block. What determined which part of the block advanced was the darkest fabric: the black, the navy, and the purple. In Block 3, the pure violet also stood out.

This led me to design *Starry Variation*. I set myself these rules: use one warm pure color, one cool dark, and a variety of light to medium cools. Within this set of fabrics, what should dominate is the warm pure and the cool dark. This is an experiment you can do with any complicated block (it has to have enough pieces so that you can emphasize different parts). I have provided below the patterns for a 10" *Joseph's Coat* block. Try it yourself if you want to after doing Worksheets 13 and 14.

24

◆ TIME OUT TO EXPERIMENT
Do Worksheets 13 and 14 to help you understand color dominance.

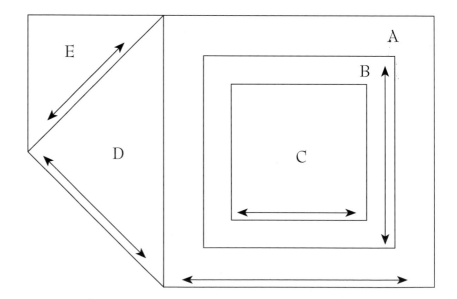

Add 1/4" seam allowances to all templates.

CHAPTER 7

◆ Background and Foreground ◆

The background is just as important to a quilt as the foreground. When designing, think of the entire quilt as your design area. Don't allow yourself to think only in terms of individual blocks of different designs and color combinations. Tie the blocks together and into the background.

If we are aware that the background is important, we can avoid making quilts where the picture is simply superimposed on that background. We want to blend background and foreground together. Using what we know about color can help us do this.

Positive and Negative Space

You may refer to the foreground and background as positive and negative space. Positive space is the foreground. It is the part of the quilt that is the main design, the part that makes a statement. It carries the main theme of the quilt.

Negative space is the background of the quilt, the area you don't want to emphasize. You shouldn't ignore the negative space, but you should treat it gently. Don't make it too busy. Remember, it's there to support the foreground. You don't want it to die, to be too dull, so you have to give it some life. And you want it to tie into the foreground. Since it helps create the atmosphere and the mood of the quilt, the background should work with the foreground.

Light Advances on Dark & Dark Advances on Light

The same design seems different when the background is altered. Any light color will advance on a dark background; any dark color will advance on a light background. This is because of contrast of value.

Black and white are the most dramatic examples of dark and light backgrounds. Black makes pure colors sing. It makes a wonderful background for playing with color because it makes colors seem lighter and brighter than they really are. White is quieter. It gives a light, clean, airy feeling, but the colors placed against it seem smaller and duller than they do on black. Look at *Six on Black* and *Six on White* on page 45. This pair of quilts was made as an experiment to test how black and white affect colors. The same rules were used—the six primary and secondary colors right off the color wheel, all pure, in the same proportion and position. Notice how the different backgrounds affect different colors. First, of course, the light colors stand out more on the black background and the dark colors on the white. Notice particularly the yellow and purple, the lightest and darkest colors used. Yellow, even though it is the strongest color, isn't as vivid on the white background as on the black because of contrast of value—both yellow and white are light colors. Purple, on the other hand, although a vivid color, is almost lost against the black background because of contrast of value. But, in general, the colors seem richer and more vibrant on the black background. *Colors of My Day*, p. 33, is another good example of how black enhances color and, therefore, makes as excellent background if you want a strong, vibrant quilt.

Background Colors

Medium values dilute the contrast between background and foreground and soften a quilt. Grayed colors act in the same way. And cool colors make quiet backgrounds.
Neutrals and earthtones (discussed in Chapter 9) are natural backgrounds. Any color which has little strength, whether because of value, warmth, or intensity can become a quiet, receding background.

Add Interest to the Background

Remember that we want the background or negative space to be interesting, to support the foreground, so we want to give it as much life as we can without changing its subordinate status. There are several ways we can add interest to the background.

1. **Use a print.** An interesting print can enliven the background. Remember, it is the color which will determine whether the background **stays** in the background, so prints can add movement and fill space without advancing. In *King's Crown* on page 42, all of the background space is made out of prints, small and beige, but varied in value. The print variety gives the background interest. In *Pine View* on page 33, all of the background fabric is varied for interest, yet color, intensity, and value keep it clearly in the background.

2. **Use a large print.** As with any fabric, it is color rather than print size which will make it the background, and a large print adds texture.

3. **Use interesting or elaborate quilting.** Quilting can add texture and detail without adding color or affecting the background's status as negative space.

4. **Repeat a color from the positive space.** It helps to unify the quilt if you repeat in the background a color found somewhere else in the quilt. Take yellow as an example. If you use a brilliant yellow fabric in the foreground, repeat it elsewhere in a minor way—smaller in size or less striking in color. This gives the quilt movement because the viewer's eye is carried from one yellow to the other. Isolated color should have echoes somewhere in the quilt. Try to repeat every color somewhere in some way.

◆ TIME OUT TO EXPERIMENT
Do Worksheet 15 to help you understand black and white as background.

CHAPTER 8

◆ Add the Third Dimension ◆

Quilts are two-dimensional. This means they are flat and without depth. Quilters over the centuries have accepted the challenge of creating the illusion of a third dimension in their quilts. Famous traditional patterns such as *Baby's Blocks*, *Attic Windows* and *Log Cabin* exemplify ways in which quilters have overcome the two-dimensional quality of quilts by designing blocks that give them depth.

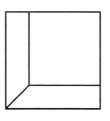
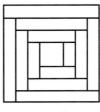

Baby's Blocks   *Attic Windows*   *Log Cabin*

Contrast of Value Creates Depth

Contrast of value helps to give a quilt depth. A mistake beginning quilters frequently make is to forget to include multiple values in their quilts. A variety of values gives a quilt life. Look at *Garden Windows* on page 41. It is made with the simple *King's X* block, but because of skillfully positioned light and dark fabrics, it gives the illusion that we are looking through windows.[15]

Warm-Cool Contrast Creates Depth and Distance

Color, too, can help achieve the illusion of depth in quilts. Or it can ruin your best-laid plans if you don't realize how color affects depth perception. We've discussed how warm colors advance more than cool, pure more than dull, and dark more than pale. We know that light colors stand out against dark backgrounds and vice versa. If we add to these color principles more information that we already know, it will enable us to create the illusion of depth in our quilts.

The colors we choose when we are playing with the illusion of distance in a quilt come from our knowledge of what we see in real life. The colors in the distance are vague, muted, and indistinct. The Blue Ridge Mountains are so named precisely because of the play of misty blues, purples, and greens fading into the distance over multiple mountain tops.

If you want to suggest distance or space, choose muted tones for the distant areas. Since cool colors recede, use them to suggest distance, too. Because of our knowledge of reality, we "read" an area as far away if it is dull, pale, and blue, even if it is simply a part of an abstract design. Blues suggest sky, and sky is traditionally in the background. Choose for the fore-ground or positive space strong colors (warm and pure) that attract the eye of the viewer.[16]

Look at *Pine View* on page 33 in quiet, toned-down colors. Note particularly the way in which the background is handled. Because of the block design, earth and sky intermingle, creating a design problem. This is solved by making the negative space pale and muted,

27

suggesting distance, with sky and earth flowing into one another. The positive space is done in darker and stronger colors, although no color in the quilt is particularly vibrant.

Pine View is a pictorial quilt, one in which there are realistic objects (however stylized) against a background. This helps the viewer "see" the foreground and background of the picture. But the illusion of background and foreground works even in an abstract design such as *Open Ended* on page 40. The modified *Baby's Blocks* seem to float in front of the sky because of value and intensity. The pale, grayed stripe recedes while the strong, warm colors of the boxes advance, creating the illusion of depth.

When we understand how color affects the illusion of depth, we can combine it with limitless designs to make quilts appear three-dimensional.

A Source of Light

Another way to alter the two-dimensional quality of a quilt is to play with light. You can pretend as you design that light is coming from somewhere either outside the quilt or within it. Then you can plan the positions of light and dark fabrics around that source of light.

In *Evening Star* on page 44, the light source is within the quilt—a silver star which radiates light throughout the quilt's night sky. The quilt uses a limited analogous color scheme of blues and purples, with the only contrast in the shading from light to dark. Yet it is strong and glowing despite its simplicity. In *Cabin Door*, page 44, the light streams through the window onto the floor. Notice how the blues go from light in the window to medium as the light filters across the dark floor.

Light can seem to come from outside or behind your quilt and glow through or sparkle from within a dark quilt as we saw in *Compromise* on page 37. It can enhance a pictorial quilt or an abstract design. It's a useful concept to play with and worthy of experimentation.

Shadows and Highlights

In reality, highlights appear opaque, so to create them, choose light values of high intensity. They are never tints of the object's color (that would be too pale), but are stronger in intensity, almost exaggerations of the color. Choose the color of a highlight from the next higher adjacent color on the wheel.

When considering shadows, remember that they are not just gray or black but have tinges of color, usually a color close to that of the object they reflect. They have a transparent feeling about them, so use soft, grayed colors, weak in intensity. Use shades of the object's color or of the next lower color on the wheel to denote shadow as was done in *Open Ended* (p. 40), where the darkest shadow is a shade of violet, the next lower color on the wheel next to red-violet.

TIME OUT TO EXPERIMENT
Do Worksheet 16 to help you understand depth, distance, light, and shadow.

Transparency

The Three Formulas

The illusion of transparency in a quilt is usually an effect you set out to achieve. Rarely do you just happen upon it. Any block in which two elements overlap provides room to work with transparency. The three formulas for achieving the illusion are shown in Figures 3, 4, and 5 on page 46 for your referral as we discuss them.

In the first, choose any three values of one color, using the medium where you want the fabrics to seem to overlap. *Matter of Choice* on page 41 is a lovely example of this simple formula. The simple monochromatic design looks as though a deep wine swath is laid over the pink fabric. But no fabric overlay is used. Instead, darker and darker strips of the same color laid side by side achieve an optical illusion. If you go from a light pink to a dark wine, where they overlap should be a medium rose. The formula works with any color.

A second way to achieve a transparent effect is to use three analogous colors on the color wheel. The two outside colors are the colors to be overlaid. Where they overlap, use the middle color. Because we know that a mixture of blue and yellow, for example, produces green, the illusion works.

In the third method, you may use any two colors. They may be as different as the exact opposites, two complements. Where they overlap, use a darker shade of one of the colors. If you are mixing warm and cool colors, the illusion seems to work better if the dark is a shade of the warm color.

Mist and Sheer Overlay

Usually when trying for transparency, you combine colors of the same intensity: pure colors together, pastel together, and so on. However, if you want a veiled or misty effect, select a paler or grayer version of whatever is the middle color in the formulas above. This gives the illusion of a sheer color laid over a bright one and suggests a feeling of mist.

Combining Formulas

Landscape II, page 45, uses all of the above methods as the several triangles overlap each other. At the top, where green overlaps pale yellow, I chose to use a yellow-green (three analogous colors). This is also a pale color, giving a misty effect. At the bottom, red and violet overlap, and I chose a dark value of a red-violet where they overlap, combining the second and third formulas. In the middle, there is a point where red-violet and blue overlap, and there I used violet. This quilt is full of overlapping elements and is, thus, a good example of transparent illusion.

The illusion of tranparency frequently does not show until the fabric is pasted or pieced and ironed. It seems to need a crisp edge to help the eye. Also, remember as you work that transparency is a long distance illusion, best unanalyzed by the viewer, simply to be enjoyed as a visual gift from the quiltmaker. And it's such fun to play with!

TIME OUT TO EXPERIMENT
Do Worksheets 17 and 18 to help you understand transparency.

CHAPTER 9
◆ Neutrals and Earthtones ◆

Neutrals

The true neutrals in color theory are black, white, and gray. These are the achromatics we discussed in Chapter 3, the non-colors that go with any color.

To these true neutrals, quilters can add the pale beiges and creams of muslin and related pale browns. We deal with them as if they are white, as if they are non-colors, as if they are background; and we can discuss them as if they are neutrals, too.

Earthtones

Earthtones play as great a part in quiltmaking as they do in our lives. We are, of course, surrounded by earthtones, and they are naturally soft and soothing. In nature, the browns, beiges, and rusts of the earth soften and act as background for the vivid blue of the sky, green of the grass and trees, and vibrant hues of the flowers. Earthtones do the same thing in quilts. Use them to tone down and soften a quilt.

Not all earthtones are always completely neutral. Rust, for example, is a strong color with lots of red-orange in it and can be too strong to remain neutral in a quilt. However, it is still less dominant than its pure versions—orange and red-orange. Brown is neutral and quiet because it is colorless in feeling (however, the more red it contains, the closer it gets to rust and the stronger it becomes).

In general, however, earthtones act to soften color contrast. You can put an earthtone next to a color to reduce its brilliance or substitute an earthtone for the stronger color.[17] Either will mute a quilt and make it more subtle in color.

Remember that a tone is a grayed version of any color. So the term *tone down* means to add gray. Neutrals, especially grays, and dull earthtones dilute the contrast between vibrant colors and soften color contrasts. A quilt made mostly in earthtones is a quiet, restful quilt. The *Thousand Pyramids* on page 43 combines browns, beiges, and rusts with a variety of other colors in small amounts for spark. It frequently sets up strong light-dark contrast, but the predominantly neutral colors gives it a quiet feeling.

Homespun Revisited on page 42 is another earthtone quilt. It is a collection of antique blocks put together with new sashing and border and made entirely of plaids and checks. There isn't one solid fabric in the quilt. Yet because the colors are soft and neutral, the viewer isn't overwhelmed by the many plaids. It is color that dictates the strength of the quilt, not the prints in the individual fabrics.

Neutrals make good backgrounds. *King's Crown* on page 42 is a quiet quilt. By using in the background a variety of beige and gray prints, I kept the contrast low yet created some activity in the negative space. The wines and dark browns in the positive space, although the strongest design elements in the quilt and in the strongest colors, are actually both grayed versions of their pure colors. Contrast is really limited to the variety of values.

◆

TIME OUT TO EXPERIMENT
Do Worksheet 19 to help you understand neutrals and earthtones.

30

CHAPTER 10

◆ Use Color for Special Effects ◆

Traditionally, artists use a particular color for one of three reasons:

        its visual effect

        its emotional effect

        its symbolic effect

Let's see what this means. Take red, for example. The artist might use red because it is bright and attracts the eye of the viewer. That is its visual effect. Or, she might use red because it is exciting and stimulating. That is its emotional effect. Then again, she might use it because it symbolizes courage, a message she wants to convey. That is its symbolic effect.

You may be oriented more one way than the other. And you probably will use colors for different purposes at different times in different quilts. But knowing what the effects of a color are and that they are inter-related helps you convey the mood or message you want.

Use Colors for Visual Effects

It's fun to be aware of and use colors for their visual effects on the viewer:

        The blues and greens are soothing and relaxing, light and airy.

        Yellow conveys weightlessness and seems to float.

        Reds and oranges are stimulating and agitating. They attract the eye.

        Pure colors convey a feeling of bouyancy.

        Muted colors convey stability and seriousness.

Combine Color and Shape

We can't isolate our use of color from the lines of the design. We have been concentrating on color and how it affects our quilts, but really "color—all by itself—is a nebulous idea." [18] Color and line or shape support each other.[19] We quilters rely on shapes all the time; they are our mainstay. Sometimes they are our reason for making a quilt. But shapes, too, affect feelings and moods.

Just as blues are soothing, relaxed colors, so are horizontal lines. Circles and S-shaped curves are graceful and soothing, too. So are evenly-spaced, spread out designs. Therefore, soothing colors combined with these shapes and designs will increase the calm feeling a quilt elicits from the viewer.

Red, on the other hand, is an exciting, agitating color. So are broken, stacatto lines and jagged edges. These shapes affect the viewer's mood.

Vertical lines, perfectly balanced forms, and squares suggest stability and dignity. These shapes, combined with toned-down colors, give a quilt a stable, calm feeling.

Dome-shaped designs, arches, and pure colors all produce bouyant effects.

Horizontal lines denote weight and distance while vertical lines soar into lightness and height. Diagonal lines, of course, force the eye to travel across the quilt and give it movement.

Circles can also give a quilt movement.

Mixing the effects of color and shape (which we do anyway, but usually unconsciously) can communicate a complex mood or idea.

Look at some of the quilts in this book to see how shape and line affect or emphasize mood. Look at the diagonal movement in *Double Irish Chain* (p. 39) and *Open Ended* (p. 40), the upward soaring of *Pine View* (p. 33) and the stable yet upward movement of *Amish Baskets* (p. 41).

Notice in these and other quilts how shape is combined with color. Dynamic combinations may have more powerful effects than we could obtain if we didn't know how color and shape work together. This isn't mere theory. Quilters are consciously using the symbolism of shape and color to make beautiful quilts.

Although these terms may be foreign to your way of thinking about quilts, try applying them to quilts you see in shows and magazines. Study the quilts that have the greatest impact on you to see how the makers consciously used their knowledge of color and shape to elicit a desired response from the audience.

Use Colors for Emotional Effects

Colors affect mood. There is established scientific evidence to verify how colors affect people. Psychologists have gotten us to brighten our hospitals, schools, children's rooms, and clothing because color affects mood. These are the moods different colors evoke, according to several color experts:

blue	placidity, relaxation, passivity, coldness
red	excitement, agitation, animation, passion, gravity
green	tranquility, hope, decay, jealousy
yellow	bouyancy, thoughtfulness, aggressiveness
pure colors	bouyancy
pastel colors	gracefulness, light, airiness[20]

Notice from the list above that the mood a color conveys can vary. For example, yellow can be bouyant or aggressive, green can be tranquil or decadent. Mood from color is subjective. It is colored by the viewer's experiences as well as preferences and by the context in which the quilter couches it. Yet, in general, certain moods are evoked by certain colors, and we quilters can use this knowledge of general color effects to make our quilts do what we want them to do.

Because, after all, we do want our quilts to **do something** or to **be something**. We usually have a purpose in mind for each quilt. We want it to lift someone's spirits or be a show stopper, to sooth or intrigue. Whatever effect we are striving for, we must first recognize that we are striving. Then we can decide how to get there from here.

Colors and Weather

Research now verifies that weather actually affects our moods. The seasons are part of that weather pattern, and color is an important part of our perception of the seasons and weather.

Colors of My Day
by Dominie Nash.
The black background
makes the colors sing.

Pine View
by Susan McKelvey
contains contrast of
value and of intensity.

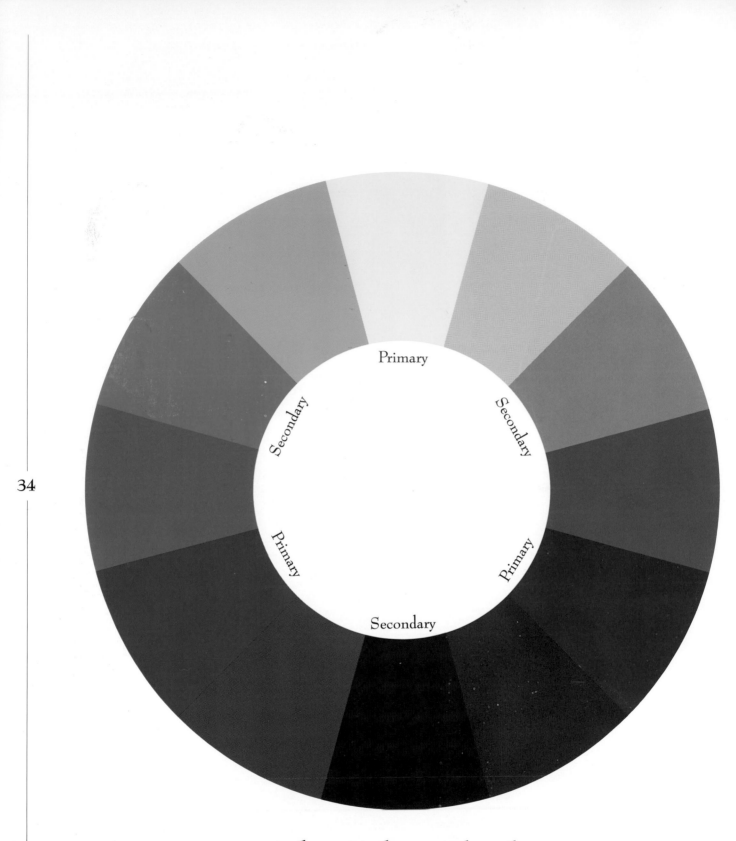

Primary

Secondary

Secondary

Primary

Primary

Secondary

The Color Wheel

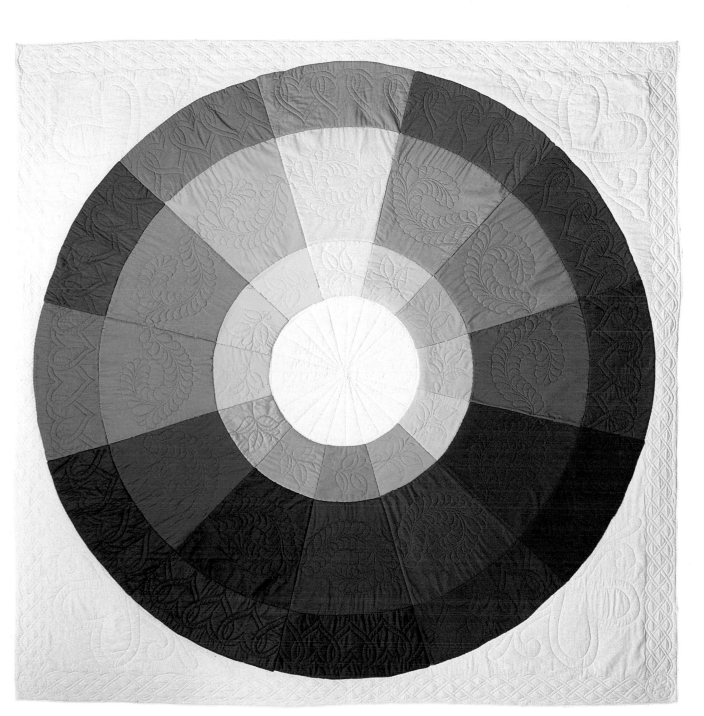

Color Wheel in Three Values
by Susan McKelvey.

Three *Joseph's Coat* Blocks in Different Colors

Block A
Achromatic
• No color • Several values

Block B
Monochromatic
• One color • Several values

Block C
Analogous
• Two colors • Several values

Starry Variation
by Susan McKelvey.
Six *Joseph's Coat* blocks colored in
different ways but using a set palette.

Three *Mexican Cross* Blocks

Block A
Monochromatic
• Includes several values.

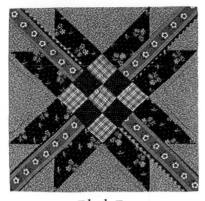

Block B
A touch of the complement
is added in the print.

Block C
A touch of the complement is added
in the pieced center 9 patch.

Compromise by Susan McKelvey contains complementary and light-dark contrast.

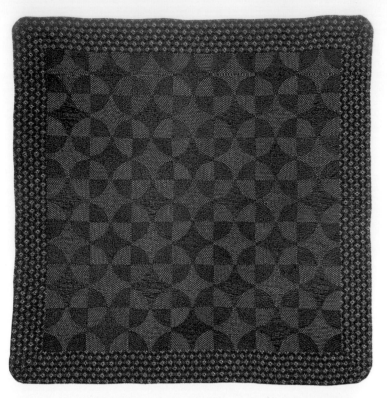

Antique **Mill Wheel**
from the collection of Dick and Ellen Swanson.
Complementary colors used equally make
this quilt vibrate.

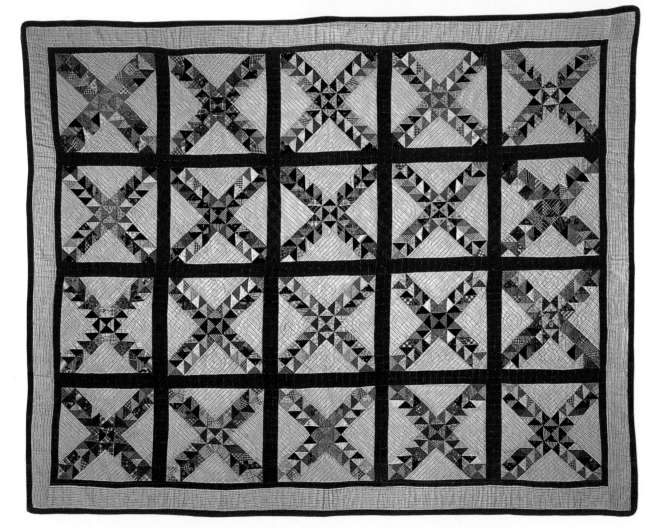

Antique *Lady of the Lake* from the collection of Dick and Ellen Swanson.
The red sashing grabs the viewer while the cool blocks become secondary.

Peony Medallion
by Anne Warner
is a good example of
complementary contrast with warm
red dominating the quilt.

Double Irish Chain from the collection of Nancy and Paul Hahn.
The warm yellow chain and red squares dominate this quilt.

Open Ended
by Susan McKelvey
uses the contrasts of intensity and value
to create the illusion of depth.

40

Mariner's Lily by Kathy Kolsevich is a dramatic quilt in warm and cool colors.

Matter of Choice by Nancy Nelson,
from the collection of Betty Martin, uses several values
of red to create the illusion of transparency.

Garden Windows
by Sue Pierce uses contrast of value to
create the illusion of looking through windows.

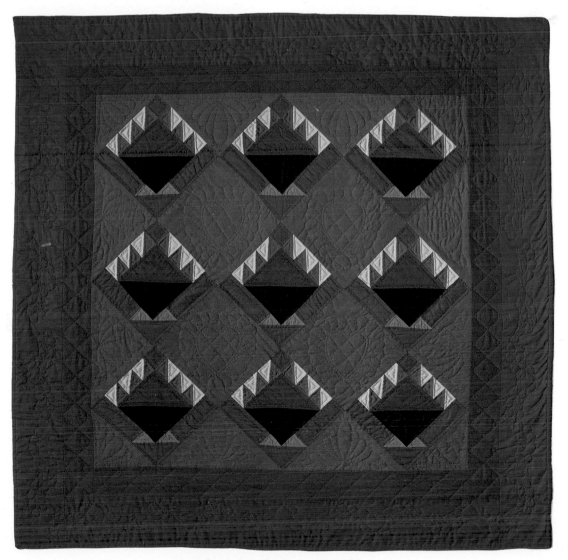

Amish Baskets by Susan McKelvey.
The connecting blocks dominate the pieced blocks because of vivid, pure color.

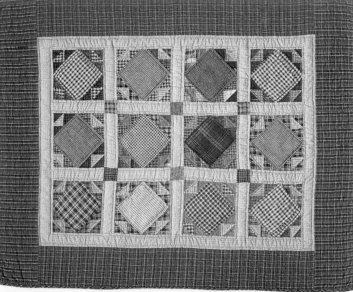

Homespun Revisited
by Susan McKelvey
is a collection of antique blocks put together
with new sashing and borders. Despite its many prints,
it is a quiet quilt because of color.

King's Crown by Susan McKelvey,
from the collection of Tom and Mary Sharp, uses neutrals to soften color contrast.

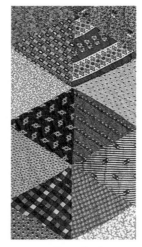

Detail of
Thousand Pyramids.
Note the colorful prints.

Antique **Thousand Pyramids** from the collection of Dick and Ellen Swanson.
Although this is an earthtone quilt, notice the many bright colors included.

Detail of **9 Patch**.
Note the busy prints.

Antique **9 Patch** from the collection of Dick and Ellen Swanson
includes many large prints but retains its soft feeling.

Cabin Door by Dominie Nash combines the traditional *Log Cabin* block with color and value to create the illusion of light streaming in the window.

Evening Star by Caryl Rae Hancock uses an analogous color scheme and light radiating from inside.

44

February Blues by Sue Pierce is done in a monochromatic color scheme but achieves texture and variety through contrast of value.

Six on Black and **Six on White**
are identical quilts by Susan McKelvey, using the same six primary and secondary colors in
the same proportions and positions but on different backgrounds.

Landscape II by Susan McKelvey,
from the collection of Leslie McKelvey, uses several methods to create the illusion of transparency.

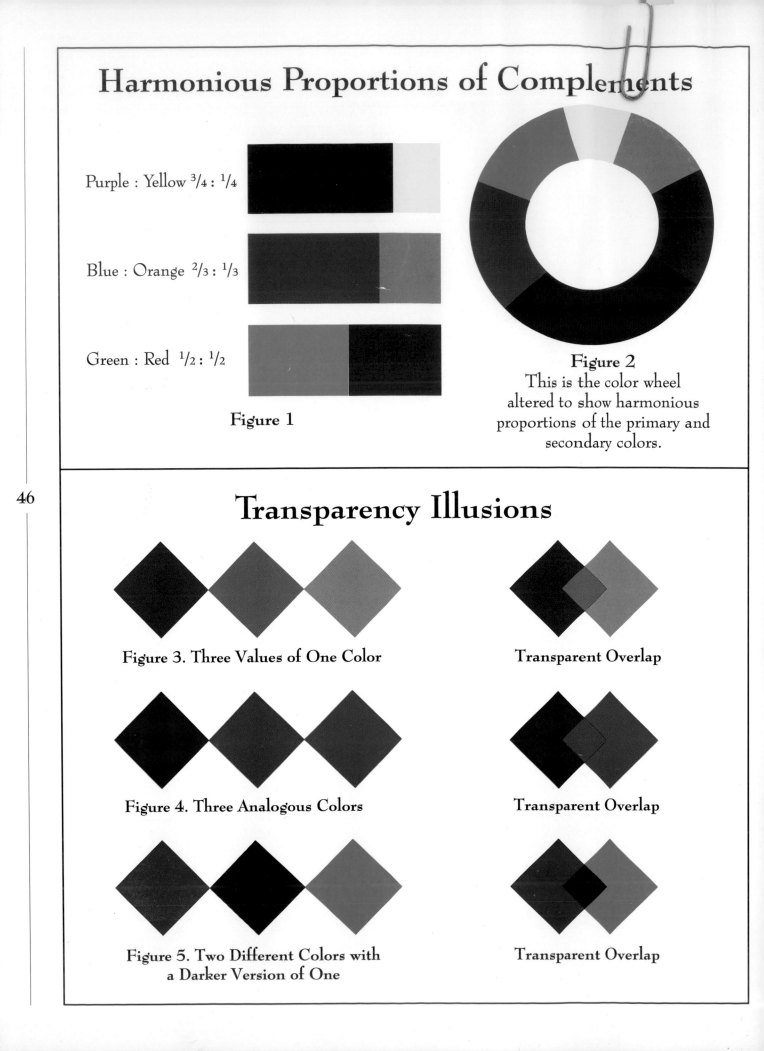

Harmonious Proportions of Complements

Purple : Yellow ³/₄ : ¹/₄

Blue : Orange ²/₃ : ¹/₃

Green : Red ¹/₂ : ¹/₂

Figure 1

Figure 2
This is the color wheel altered to show harmonious proportions of the primary and secondary colors.

Transparency Illusions

Figure 3. Three Values of One Color

Transparent Overlap

Figure 4. Three Analogous Colors

Transparent Overlap

Figure 5. Two Different Colors with a Darker Version of One

Transparent Overlap

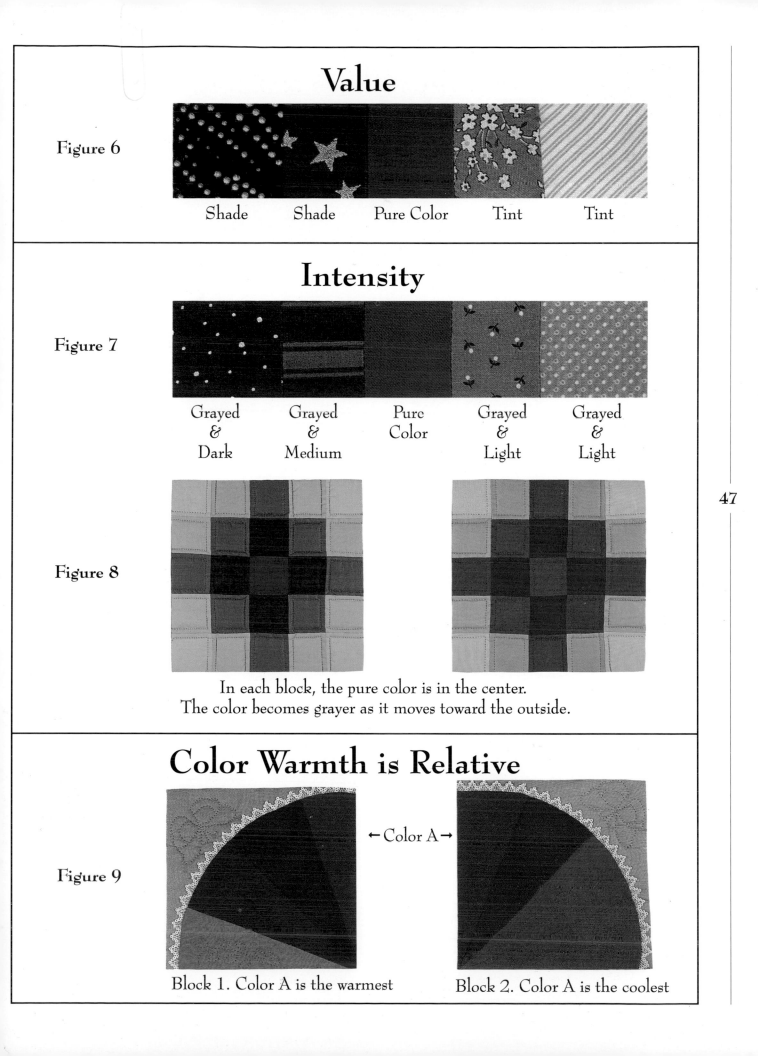

Value

Figure 6

Shade Shade Pure Color Tint Tint

Intensity

Figure 7

Grayed
&
Dark

Grayed
&
Medium

Pure
Color

Grayed
&
Light

Grayed
&
Light

47

Figure 8

In each block, the pure color is in the center.
The color becomes grayer as it moves toward the outside.

Color Warmth is Relative

← Color A →

Figure 9

Block 1. Color A is the warmest

Block 2. Color A is the coolest

Fabrics

Prints Containing Pure Colors /Intense Colors

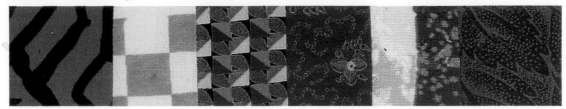

Prints of the Same Color but in Different Scales

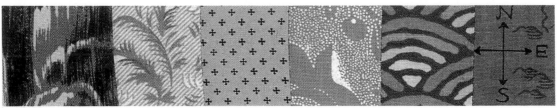

Prints Containing High Color Contrast

Prints Containing Low Color Contrast

Prints Containing Muted and Grayed Colors

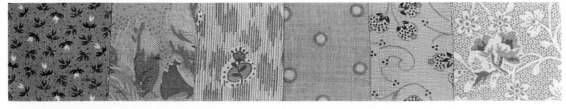

Look at the list below and either consider or jot down which colors represent which season, time of day, mood, or type of weather to you:

Seasons: Spring, Summer, Fall, Winter

Times of Day: Dawn, Morning, Afternoon, Evening, Night

Moods: Joy, Sorrow, Despair, Hope, Fear, Jealousy, Calmness

Weather: Rain, Fog, Sun, Wind, Heat, Cold

Though the specific colors you choose may differ from others' choices, they won't differ much. Our culture conditions us to relate certain colors to certain conditions. Color symbolism has become almost color cliché.

Use Colors Symbolically

One of the most fascinating aspects of color is its symbolic meaning. Color has played a part in man's symbolism for thousands of years. We learn the symbolic meanings of colors in our culture as children and use them unconsciously all of our lives. Some are from nature, some from years of tradition. In different cultures, colors may connote different ideas, but in Western culture, colors have the following symbolic meanings:

blue	sky, heaven, water
green	water, hope, spring, renewal; or jealousy and fear (these are poisonous emotions and come from the fact that the arsenic manufactured in ancient times was green and was used to poison enemies)
red	blood, courage, sacrifice
black	death, the underworld, mourning, desolation
white	purity, chastity, or surrender, cowardice
yellow	sun, wealth, or envy, treachery, cowardice
purple	royalty, authority
gray	colorlessness, flatness[21]

Colors affect us at their symbolic level because, within our culture, we are all familiar with their connotations. You sometimes may choose to work with color symbolically. Certainly patriotic quilts in red, white and blue are examples of the symbolic use of color. Wedding quilts; anniversary quilts; commemorative quilts honoring states or cities, schools or churches; all are examples of places we might use color for symbolic meaning above other considerations.

TIME OUT TO EXPERIMENT
Do Worksheets 20 and 21 to help you understand how color can be used to affect mood or communicate a symbolic message.

CHAPTER 11
◆ Apply Color Theory to Fabric ◆

Quilters cannot work directly with only color. We cannot mix our paint to blend the perfect value of a color. That is our disadvantage. We create with fabric, preprinted, predyed, and frequently multicolored within itself. That, too, is our disadvantage.

But it is our great joy, too! A love of fabric is why many of us are in quiltmaking. We are, however, subject to the whims of fashion in the palette we can buy in any given year. For many of us, therefore, this means collecting, hoarding, trading, knowing that someday that coveted fabric will be just right somewhere, in some quilt.

Amass a Varied Collection

Variety is the key to a dramatic quilt and, therefore, to amassing a useful fabric collection. Although we are primarily interested in color variety here, we need to maintain variety in the kinds of prints we buy, too. Include in your collection fabric that is different in style, layout, and scale as well as in color and value. Include some fabric from each of the categories below.

Style—There are several kinds of fabric prints:

Florals:	flowers and plants of all kinds, can be realistic or stylized
Geometrics:	designs derived from a geometric shape, includes stripes and plaids
Conversationals:	pictures of real objects or creatures
Ethnic:	designs derived from different cultures

Layout—Print designs can be laid out in different ways. They can be:

Directional:	versus non-directional
Allover:	there is more motif than background
Set:	a formal, static layout
Tossed:	motifs don't repeat at regular, consistent intervals

Scale—Prints can be in different sizes or scales.

Color Contrast within Fabric

For many of us, the real challenge lies in using color successfully. Two fabrics may be described as blue and be miles apart in value and in character. Fabrics have moods, perhaps elegant or playful, sombre or cheery. They have different kinds of color contrast going on within themselves. Within one fabric, you may frequently see several contrasts: warm-cool, light-dark, and perhaps others. Each fabric needs to be analyzed for its contribution to your quilt. Look at the fabric swatches on page 48 for examples of the different kinds of contrast.

Stand Back and Squint

Examine successful antique quilts and you'll find that our quiltmaking forebears weren't afraid to mix large prints, plaids, bright fabrics, odd fabrics. Yet the effect of all the fabrics together is not frantic. Why? Because it is color that determines how well a fabric will blend with others.

And remember, to determine color, you must stand back from a fabric (p. 20). From a distance of five feet, by squinting or removing your glasses, you lose line and see only color. In this way, you can determine whether a fabric is right for a quilt. It is sometimes difficult to convince yourself that the interaction of colors within a fabric doesn't matter, but the true test is to stand back. Only then will you see how the fabric will look in a quilt. Color is a long-distance factor.

Look at the two antique quilts on page 43. Seen as full quilts, they look soft in color, mostly browns and blues. Yet the detail photographs show how bold and varied are the actual fabrics used in the quilts. In the *9 Patch*, the connecting blocks are wild, large scale, high contrast prints and stripes, and many of the fabrics in both quilts are, in themselves, bright and busy. Yet they don't stand out in the overall quilts because from a distance, the lines are softened or lost, and only color remains.

Proportion and Scale

An entire bolt of a fabric is often so powerful that you forget that you will be using only tiny pieces of it. It is sometimes helpful to buy a quarter yard of a fabric, take it home, cut it up, and play with it before deciding to buy many yards. Or in the shop, cover some of it up with other fabrics to "cut it down to size."

Prints as Background

As we mentioned in Chapter 7, using prints for backgrounds is a wonderful way to give spark to a quilt. When considering whether a print will make a good background, look at its color, not the size of the print. It needs to recede if it is to be background. Therefore, it needs to be low in contrast, cool in color, neutral, grayed or pale. Pile the fabrics you are considering together and stand back to determine which will recede and which advance. The color comes first; the print will follow.

Asking yourself questions about fabrics may seem artificial at first, but it will become automatic with time. And it is what you have been doing all along, perhaps without knowing what questions to ask.

Your fabrics are your color palette. Painters can mix their colors with ease. We who work in fabric must replace mixing with searching and amassing a collection full of variety.

Although color theory is easier to apply to solid fabrics because they fit easily into color categories, it also applies to prints. A print fabric has an overall effect—it "reads" as bright or pale, dark or light, warm or cool, just as the solids do.

You should be able to mix fabrics and know what they will do in a quilt and why. If you practice in shops, with your friends, and with your own collection of fabrics, soon you will be able to analyze fabrics and what's happening within them. This, in turn, will help you combine them into stunning quilts.

TIME OUT TO EXPERIMENT
Do Worksheet 22 to help you sort out different kinds of fabric.

CHAPTER 12

◆ Retain Your Personal Color Style ◆

Color preference is subjective. We quilters frequently work in colors we love. At first, we work entirely with colors we love, surrounding ourselves with these colors in our homes and clothing. There are also colors we choose **not** to deal with. It is difficult to force ourselves to go outside our color preferences. I find it difficult to resist certain colors when planning a project and going through my fabric stash. Unless I exercise extreme self-discipline, all of my quilts will resemble each other in color scheme.

Having to make quilts for others forces us to go beyond our limited personal preferences. Perhaps you remember a promised quilt for an aunt or a cousin in colors to match their preferences, not yours, which greatly challenged your resources. This challenge was good, pushing you beyond your personal limits. But it still limited you, this time to someone else's color choices.

Each of us has these color preferences. They lead to our style; they are our joy. A study of color theory is not meant to take that away. It is meant to supplement these personal preferences with knowledge of what our favorite colors and others do to each other when combined in our work, how they intereact and why.

Open New Vistas

Your early quilts represent your **own** color principles, your flair. But universal principles will help enliven your work and expand your choices. The information and projects in *Color for Quilters II* should enable you to analyze your own work, correct your problems, appreciate others' quilts, and, hopefully, advance the quality of quiltmaking. It is meant to strengthen your creativity, not to stifle it.

Dare to make mistakes, dare to discard, to waste fabric, and to try again. Be willing to spend time, too—time, that precious commodity—in experimenting, in doing the Worksheets in this book. Your grasp of color theory will increase only with practice. Knowledge can become internalized and intuitive only gradually, through use.

Studying color and thus being able to analyze quilts and fabrics freed me, set me soaring toward new possibilities. It opened new vistas and made the process of quiltmaking more exciting. It can do the same for you!

A knowledge of color principles need not override your creativity or your pleasure in your own color sense. Rules are made to be broken, and individuality should speak through every endeavor. Take theory and make it your own. May it open new vistas for you, too.

TIME OUT TO EXPERIMENT
Do Worksheet 23 to record your own color style.

◆
The Workbook

We hear, and we forget,
We see, and we remember,
We do, and it is ours forever.

The best way to learn a subject such as color is to take fabric and **play** with it. In this Workbook you will find a Worksheet based on each important color term we have discussed, each containing specific directions and page references back to the text of the book. By working your way through these Worksheets, you will gain experience with color theory and see how it applies to quilts.

The Worksheets are designed to be done in the pasteup method, using actual fabric. You may use colored pencils or markers for some, if the fabric pieces would be too small. But coloring is often a pale imitation of what you will achieve with fabric. Fabric pasteup gives you a much truer vision of what a finished quilt would actually look like.

When you have done all the Worksheets, you will have a set of samples done in your own fabrics to keep as a reference.

Many of the Worksheets would be good projects to do in actual fabrics, making small quilts for pillows or wallhangings. When you want to continue your color study, use the Worksheets as jumping off points. All of them grew out of exercises I have my students do in workshops.

Best of luck and have a grand time!

The Color Wheel

Refer to pages 8 and 9 and the color wheel on page 34.

Pasteup the twelve colors of the color wheel, matching as closely as possible the sample wheel on page 34. Use solids, prints, or a combination. It helps to begin by putting yellow and purple in the correct positions and working out from those two colors. Trace any wedge to make a template.

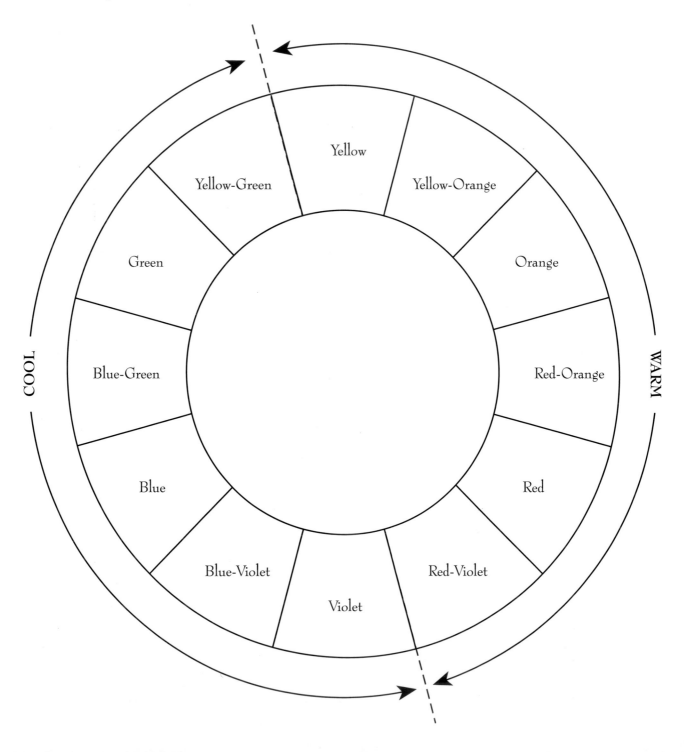

Value and Intensity

Value: Refer to page 10 and Figure 6 on page 47.

You can change the pure colors on the color wheel by adding either black or white. In the charts below, pasteup two examples of value gradations from your own fabric collection. Start with the pure color in the center square and add several shades on the left and several tints on the right.

Shade	Shade	Pure Color	Tint	Tint

Shade	Shade	Pure Color	Tint	Tint

Intensity: Refer to pages 10 and 11 and Figure 7 on page 47.

You can change the pure colors on the color wheel by diluting their intensity or graying them. This tones them down and makes them quieter. In the charts below, pasteup two examples of diluted intensity. Start with the pure color in the center. From your fabrics, choose grayed versions of that color; use any values; consider only grayness. Put the darker ones on one side and the lighter on the other.

Grayed	Grayed	Pure Color	Grayed	Grayed

Grayed	Grayed	Pure Color	Grayed	Grayed

Achromatic - Monochromatic
Polychromatic - Analogous   *Worksheet 3*

Refer to pages 11 and 12 and the *Joseph's Coat* blocks on page 36.

Below are four blocks. Design different color schemes for each, using the four color combinations described in Chapter 3. When you are finished, stand back and notice how different the same block looks when pieced in different colors.

Achromatic   Monochromatic

Polychromatic   Analogous

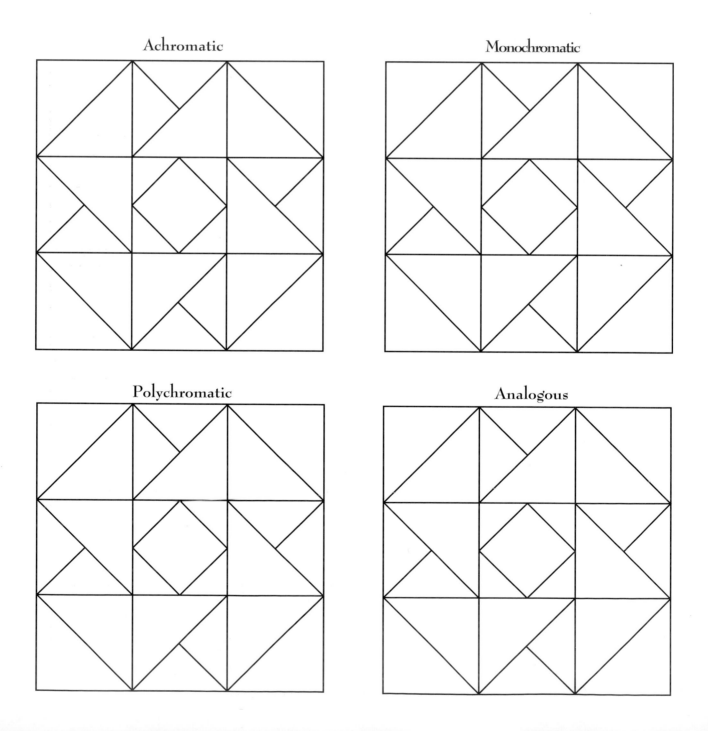

Complements

Refer to page 14 and the color wheel on page 34.

Below is a chart listing the complements, with the cool colors on the left and the warm colors on the right. Refering to the color wheel on page 34, pasteup fabric samples of the pairs of complementary contrasts. Use any value of any of the colors. Prints make good examples, too. Just be sure the prints "read" as the color from five feet away.

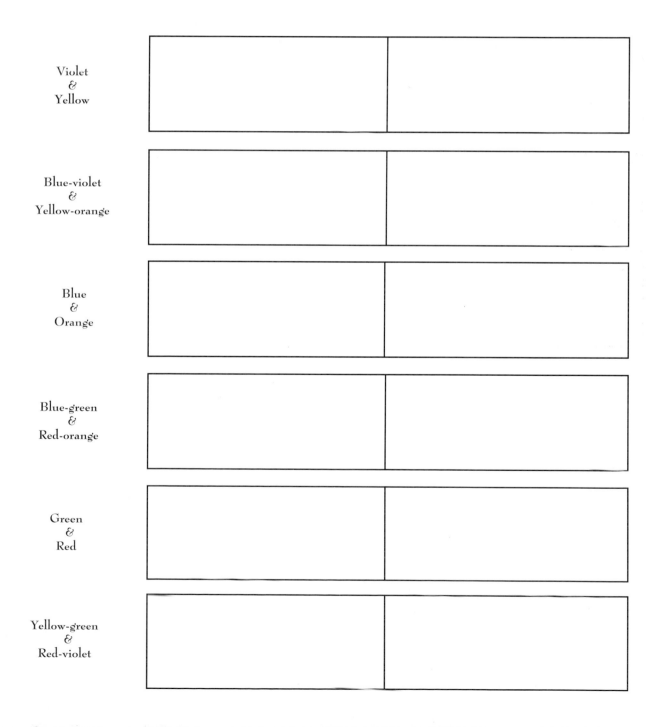

Violet
&
Yellow

Blue-violet
&
Yellow-orange

Blue
&
Orange

Blue-green
&
Red-orange

Green
&
Red

Yellow-green
&
Red-violet

Harmonious Color Combinations Patterns

Worksheet 5

Refer to page 15 and the color wheel on page 34.

Below are patterns for triangles and tetrads to lay over the color wheel on page 34 to find harmonious color combinations you may not have considered.

    Use plastic template material or heavy cardboard to make your figures. If your material is translucent, trace the shapes onto it and cut out. If not, trace the shapes onto tracing paper, glue the paper onto the cardboard, and cut out. Label the figures as these are labeled. Turn to Worksheet 6 and play with the color harmonies.

Patterns for Triangles &
Tetrads to Lay over the Color Wheel

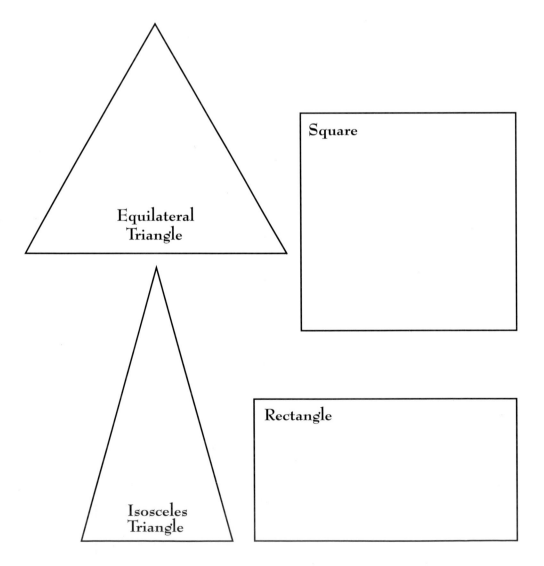

Harmonious Color Combinations

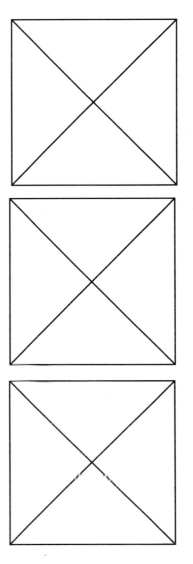

Worksheet 6

Refer to page 15 and the color wheel on page 34.

It is fun to try color combinations dictated by the triangles and tetrads because they are often truly new to you. They may force you to stretch your personal definition of harmony—and stretching your color sense is what we're all about in this book.

  Below are three triangles and three squares. Use each of the four harmonious shapes at least once. Each time, lay a triangle or tetrad on the color wheel, turn it until you find an interesting color combination, then find fabrics that resemble those colors and paste them up below. Label each example for reference. A fun exercise in self-discipline is to choose your least favorite color on the wheel and, using one of the triangles or tetrads, find colors that are harmonious with it.

3 Color Combinations   4 Color Combinations

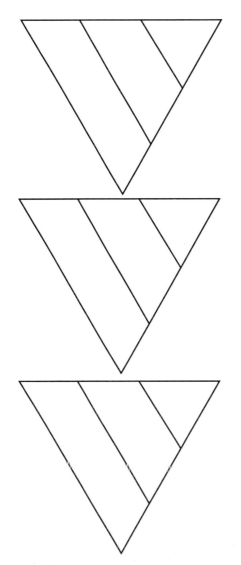

Complementary Contrast *Worksheet 7*

Refer to pages 16 and 17 and the quilts discussed there.

Below are four blocks. Design complementary color schemes for each one, following the directions below the blocks. The exercise works best if you design each block one at a time without worrying about the next block.

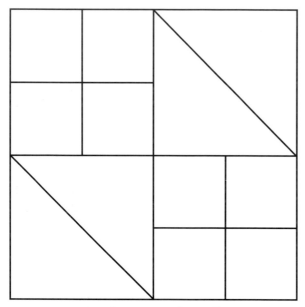

Complements Used Equally
Choose two complements and one background neutral color.
Use the complements equally.

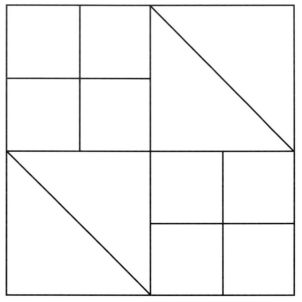

Complements Used Unequally
Use the same fabrics as in the first block, but use a lot of one complement and just a little of the other.

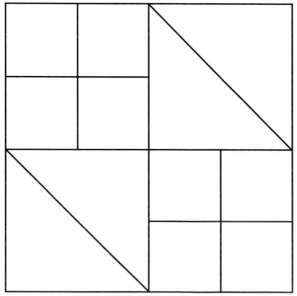

Complements Used Unequally with Several Values
To the three fabrics you used above, add several values of one of the complements. You might replace the neutral with these.

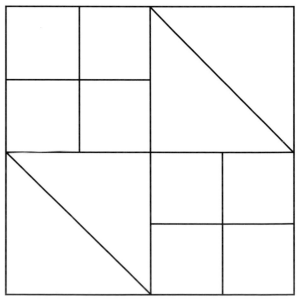

Complements Used Unequally with Several Values
To the three fabrics you used above, add several values of the other complement. You might replace the neutral with these.

Light-Dark Contrast or
Contrast of Value

Worksheet 8

Refer to page 18 and the quilts discussed there.

Below are four blocks. Design color schemes for each one, following the directions below the blocks.

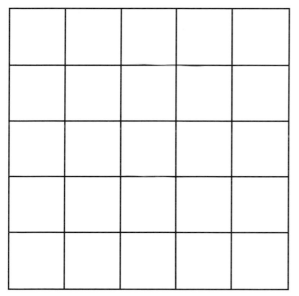

Light & Dark Next to Each Other
Use three fabrics: 1 light, 1 dark, 1 neutral. Place
the light and dark next to each other.

Light & Dark Separated by Medium
Add several other medium values between
the 2 you used in Block 1. Arrange the
design from light to dark.

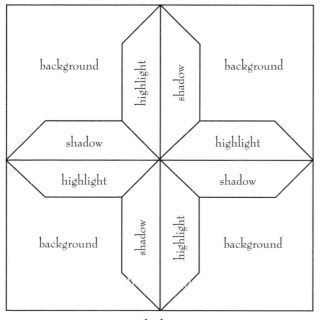

Shadow
Choose 3 values of the same or different colors.
Use the darkest for the shadow, the purest for the highlight,
and the lightest for background.

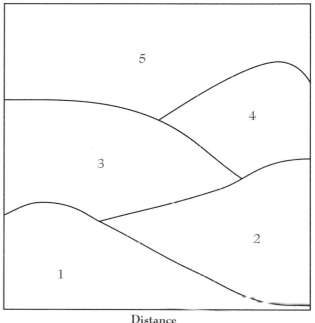

Distance
Choose five greens and blues of different value and
intensity. Arrange and pasteup from dark and pure in
the foreground to light and dull in the background.

Warm-Cool Contrast   *Worksheet 9*

Which Colors Recede and Which Advance? Refer to *Starry Variation* on page 36.

For this exercise, you will use the same fabrics in all of the blocks. Choose 4 or 5 fabrics:
1 warm pure color, 1 cool dark value, and several cool light values. Design one block at
a time; don't worry about how other blocks will look. When you finish with the first block,
go on to the others, placing the warm pure color and the cool dark in different places in each
block. When you are finished, stand back and see how this placement affects the design.
Decide on the sashing color last, depending upon how much you want it to stand out.

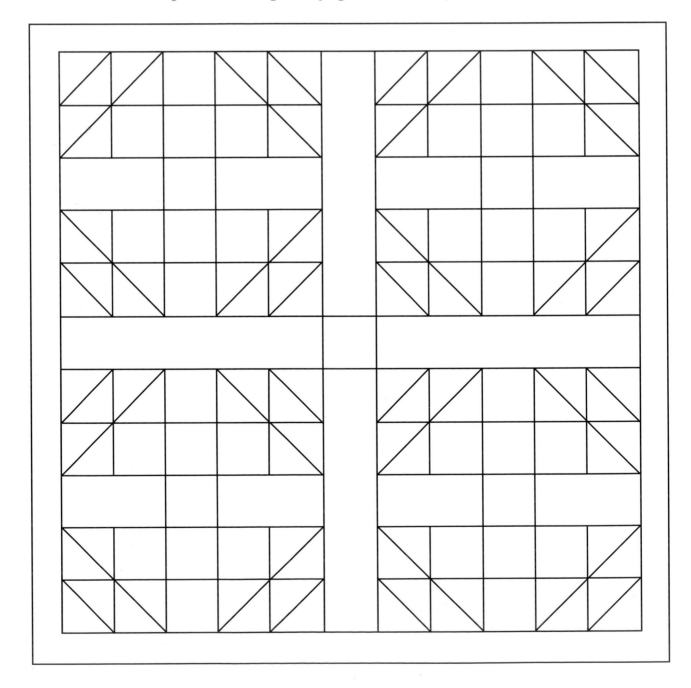

Color Warmth is Relative   *Worksheet 10*

Refer to page 20 and Figure 9 on page 47.

Below are four fan blocks, each containing four spaces. Design two at a time. For the top two blocks, choose seven analogous colors, starting anywhere on the color wheel. For this exercise, it is easiest to stay close to the pure colors on the wheel. Place the middle fabric of the seven as directed, then work out from it in two directions. In Block 1, it will be the warmest color, but in Block 2, it will be the coolest. Try the exercise again in Blocks 3 and 4, using different colors.

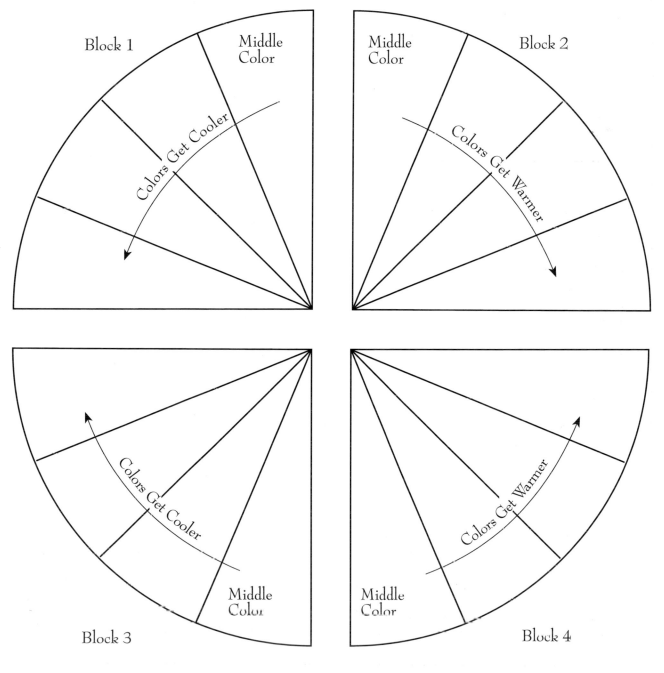

Colors Have Different Strengths

Refer to pages 21 and 22 and Figures 1 and 2 on page 46.

Below are four blocks in which to play with the concept of color strength. For each block, follow the directions below the blocks.

Use pure yellow and violet together in harmonious proportion. Use several values of each if you want.

Use pure yellow and several other pure colors together in equal amounts.

Use pure yellow and several other colors together, using very little yellow.

Use any colors together, trying to observe the proportions of color strength.

Intensity and Simultaneous Contrast

Intensity   Refer to page 22 and Figure 8 on page 47.

For the block below, choose a pure color and four toned-down versions of it. Try to find several different values of grayed colors. Pasteup as shown with the pure color in the center, then going from dark to light from the center outward.

lightest	light	medium	light	lightest
light	medium	dark	medium	light
medium	dark	pure	dark	medium
light	medium	dark	medium	light
lightest	light	medium	light	lightest

Simultaneous Contrast   Refer to page 22.

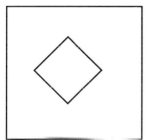 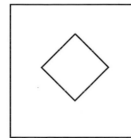 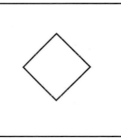 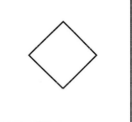

Try two of the samples of simultaneous contrast in complementary colors and two in gray. For the first two blocks, choose a pair of pure complements and reverse them on each. For the second two blocks, put gray on two different pure colors. From a distance, see how the colors affect each other. The color changes will be subtle.

What Colors Dominate? *Worksheet 13*
Design a Block Using
What You Know about Color

Design a *Trip Around the World* block, using five colors. Include warm-cool contrast and contrast of value. Your goal is to make the eight squares marked stand out. To play before pasting, cut eight squares of each color and rearrange them on the block until you find which dominates. Put it in the eight squares marked. Add the other colors to make an attractive design.

		Dominant Color		
	Dominant Color		Dominant Color	
Dominant Color				Dominant Color
	Dominant Color		Dominant Color	
		Dominant Color		

Analyzing the Quilts for Kinds of Contrast

Go through the book and choose four quilts to analyze. Then fill in the chart below.

	1	2	3	4
Quilt Name				
Colors in the Quilt				
Which Color/s Dominate?				
Parts of the Quilt which Stand Out (block? border? lattice? other?)				
Type/s of Contrast in the Quilt				
Dominant Type of Contrast				

Light & Dark Backgrounds *Worksheet 15*
White and Black Backgrounds

Refer to pages 25 and 26.

For the block below, choose ten bright, clear (almost pure) colors, some dark, some light. Cut two triangles of each color. Pasteup following directions, using each color once on black and once on white. Stand back and notice how different the same colors look on the different backgrounds, particularly the darkest and lightest colors. Remember that light colors stand out more on dark backgrounds and vice versa because there is contrast of value.

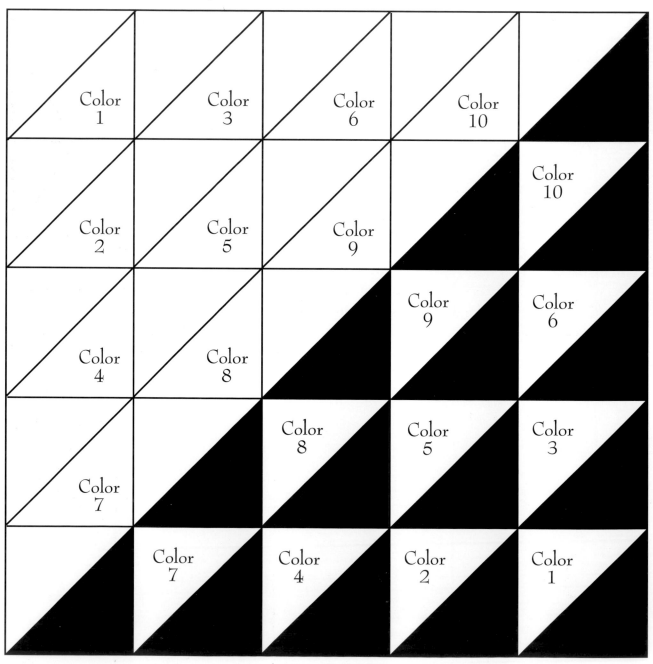

Depth, Distance, Light and Shadow

Refer to pages 27 and 28 and the *Thousand Pyramids* on page 43.

Using what you have learned about color dominance, make some areas of this *Thousand Pyramids* design come forward and some recede.

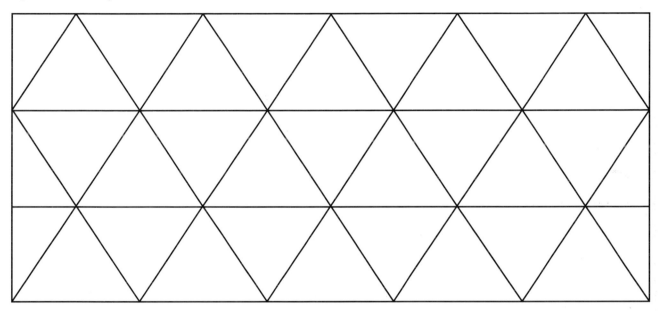

Using what you have learned about color and dominance, combine as many colors as you want in the *Baby's Blocks* design below, making it appear as if the light is shining onto the blocks from above with the darkest shadow on the right as in the sample block.

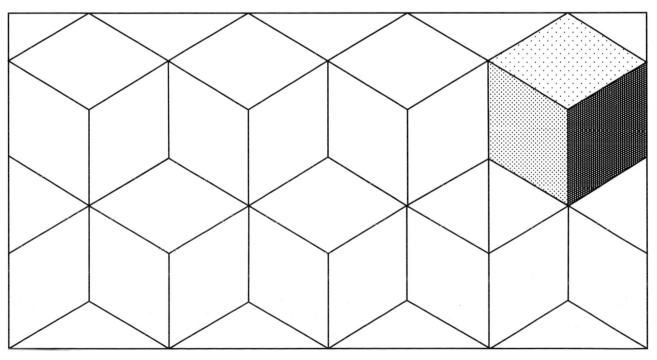

Transparency

Refer to page 29 and Figures 3, 4, and 5 on page 46.

In the three sets of hearts below, pasteup your own examples of the three ways to achieve the illusion of transparency with fabric. Follow the directions for each set.

Three Values of One Color

Choose three values of one color, putting the medium value in the middle space.

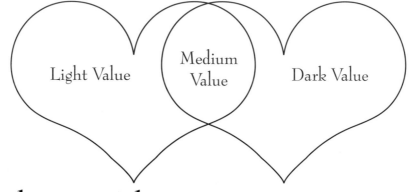

Three Analogous Colors

Choose three analogous colors of the same intensity. Paste them up in the order they appear on the color wheel, with the middle one in the middle space.

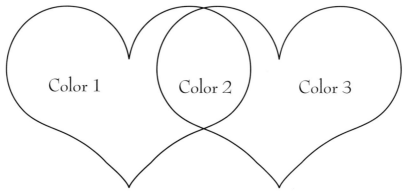

A Darker Version of One Color

Choose any two colors of the same intensity and a darker version of one of them (usually a dark of the warmer color works well). Paste them up with the dark color in the middle space.

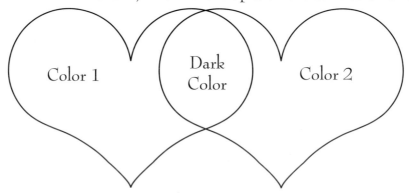

Transparency

Refer to page 29 and Figures 3, 4, and 5 on page 46.

The block below is a good one on which to play with transparency. Use any of the methods for creating transparency. Pretend that the diamonds overlap both the center square and the outer background.

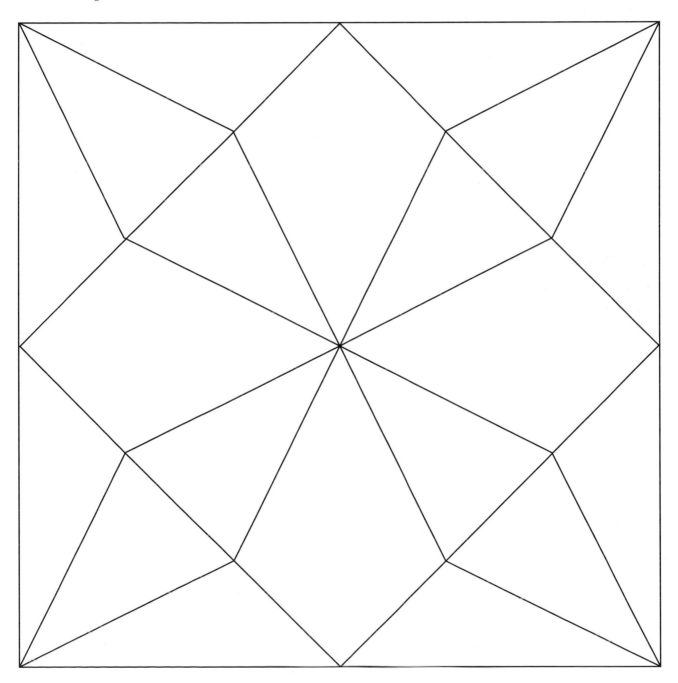

Neutrals and Earthtones *Worksheet 19*

Refer to page 30 and the quilts discussed there.

On the charts below, pasteup samples of print fabrics from your collection of neutrals and earthtones. Include prints with low contrast! When judging a print's color, remember to view it from five or more feet away.

True Neutrals: Black, White and Gray

Add Quilters' Neutrals: Muslins and Pale Beiges

Earthtones: Rusts, Browns, and Beiges

Refer to pages 31, 32, and 49.

In the block below, you have the opportunity to create a mood, using what you know about color and shape. Design a traditional block or a pictorial one. Consider any of these or any other moods: soothing and relaxed, exciting and stimulating, bouyant and happy, cold and remote. When you have finished, ask friends to tell you the mood or message you've conveyed. You may be too close to the project to evaluate your success.

Refer to page 49.

In the four blocks below, use what you know about the symbolism of color to create designs which denote different symbolic messages. Use any traditional blocks or design your own. Consider these or any other themes: patriotism, royalty, hope, mourning. Ask friends to guess the message.

Refer to pages 50 and 51 and the sample fabrics on page 48.

What color is the fabric from five feet away? In color terms that is what counts. In the Charts below, pasteup examples of prints from your fabric collection, using prints both large and small, geometrics, florals, and conversationals. Test your fabrics before pasteup by examining them from a distance.

Prints Containing Pure Colors/Intense Colors

Prints of the Same Color but in Different Scales

Prints Containing High Color Contrast

Prints Containing Low Color Contrast

Prints Containing Muted and Grayed Colors

Refer to page 52.

My Favorite Colors
(I'll just pasteup some swatches!)

My Most Hated Colors
(I wonder why I don't have many samples? I could just list them.)

_____

_____

_____

Colors on the Wheel I Don't Use Much but I Don't Hate.
(Perhaps I should try to use them?)

_____

_____

My Plans and Goals in Color Study
(Perhaps I should try something new, expand my horizon. How?)

_____

_____

_____

◆ Effects Colors Have on Each Other ◆

Action	Effect
Use an achromatic color scheme	easy, safe, can be dull
Use a monochromatic color scheme	easy, safe, soothing
Use an analogous color scheme	easy, safe, soothing
Use a polychromatic color scheme	exciting, active
Use cool colors	calm, soothing
Use warm colors	stimulating, exciting
Use warm and cool colors together	strong, exciting
Use warm colors in the background	it becomes foreground
Use cool colors in the foreground	it becomes background
Use complements together	stimulating, strong
Use complements equally	vibrating, hard to look at
Use complements unequally	strong but harmonious
Use pure colors	strong, exciting
Use toned-down colors	soft, soothing
Use light & dark values right next to each other	strong, vibrant
Go gradually from light to dark values	softens contrast
Use several kinds of contrast together	strong, vibrant
Use gray with a color	it takes on the cast of the complement
Combine color & shape	emphasize effects of both
Echo a color in the background	balances
Add gray or separate colors with gray	neutralizes, softens
Add neutrals or separate with neutrals	neutralizes, softens
Add black or separate with black	strengthens and brightens colors
Add white or separate with white	softens colors
Use a variety of prints styles & sizes	adds texture & interest
Use lots of yellow	makes a bright quilt
Use a lot of one color next to a little of another	small area takes on color of large

◆ Glossary of Color Terms ◆

achromatic: without color

advance: to come forward

analogous: colors next to each other on the color wheel

balance: a state of stability or harmony

brilliance: the intensity or vividness of a color

chroma: another word for color, the intensity of a color on a gray scale

chromatic: pertaining to color

color: the name given to different pure colors, a distinctive, unmixable color; another word for color is *hue*

color wheel: a circle of twelve pure colors formed by mixing the three primary colors

complement: the color directly opposite a given color on the colorwheel; each color has only one complement

contrast: to set two or more things together to emphasize their differences.

  color contrast: using two or more different colors together

  contrast of value: using two or more values together; using light and dark colors together

  warm-cool contrast: using warm and cool colors together

  complementary contrast: using two complements together

  contrast of color strength: using two colors together in proportion to their strengths

  contrast of saturation: using colors of different chroma or grayness together

  simultaneous contrast: colors close together change each other

cool colors: blues and greens, the colors of sky, sea, and grass

depth: giving a two dimensional quilt a feeling of three dimensions

earth tones: the browns and beige colors of the earth

expand: when an object, because of its color, appears larger than it really is

foreground: the main focus of the design

harmony: balance of colors

  subjective harmony: a color plan that pleases you

  objective harmony: a color plan that is pleasing according to color principles

hue: the name given different distinct colors; another word for *color*

intensity: the strength of a color, its purity

monochromatic: using only one color but any number of values

mood: the feeling a quilt conveys to its viewers

movement: the viewer's eyes move over a quilt; color affects that movement

neutral: black, white, and gray (the achromatics), having no color

negative space: background; the area not emphasized

placement: where a color is on the quilt (eg.: bottom or top)

polychromatic: many colored

positive space: foreground, the quilt area emphasized

primary colors: red, yellow, and blue; the three colors from which all others are mixed

pure colors: the most intense or saturated colors (the colors on the color wheel)

quilters' neutrals: pale beiges and muslin as well as the true neutrals

recede: to appear to fade into the background

saturation: the purity or intensity of a color; pure versus grayed colors

secondary colors: orange, green, and purple: the second set of colors made by mixing the primary colors

shade: a darker value of a pure color, made by adding black

simultaneous contrast: the effect of colors upon each other when they are placed close together

spatial effect: creating an illusion of space or depth

stability: when there is little or no movement in a quilt

strength: colors have different strength and power

tertiary colors: the third set of colors on the color wheel, formed by combining primary and secondary colors

tint: a lighter value of a pure color, made by adding white

tone: a grayed version of a color, made by adding gray

value: the degree of lightness or darkness of a color

vibration: jumpiness, a feeling of movement

warm colors: reds, yellows, and oranges; the colors of fire and the sun

◆ Footnotes ◆

1. Johannes Itten, *The Elements of Color* (New York: Van Nostrand Reinhold Co., 1970), p.7.
2. There are many different color wheels used to explain color theory. The greatest difference is between pigment-based and light-based wheels. I have chosen a pigment-based wheel because it is the most familiar wheel and allows a broad explanation of complements.
3. A. H. Munsell, *A Color Notation* (Baltimore: Munsell Color Company, Inc., 1946), pp. 31-40, and Itten, p. 49.
4. Itten, p. 73. Entire discussion of harmonious triangles and tetrads.
5. Itten, p.32. Entire discussion of contrast.
6. Lucia A. Salemme, *Color Exercises for the Painter* (New York: Watson-Guptill Publications, 1970), p. 27.
7. Itten, p. 45.
8. Itten, p. 45.
9. Franklyn M. Branley, *Color from Rainbows to Lasers* (New York: Thomas Y. Crowell Company, 1978), p. 76.
10. Branley, p. 76.
11. Itten, p.61.
12. Itten, p. 61.
13. Itten, p. 55.
14. Richard G. Ellinger, *Color Sturcture and Design* (New York: Van Nostrand Reinhold Company, 1980), p. 8.
15. Susan McKelvey, *Light & Shadows* (Lafayette, CA: C & T Publishing, 1989), the entire book deals with how color affects the illusions of depth, distance, light and shadow.
16. Salemme, p. 70.
17. Salemme, p. 24.
18. Salemme, p. 147.
19. Itten, p. 75 ff.
20. Salemme, p. 152, and Itten, p. 75.
21. Ralph Fabri, *Color: A Complete Guide for Artists* (New York: Watson-Guptill Publications, 1967), p. 64.

◆ Bibliography ◆

Albers, Joseph. *The Interaction of Color*. New Haven: Yale University Press, 1975.

Birren, Faber. *Creative Color*. West Chester, PA: Schiffer Publishing, 1987.

Branley, Franklyn M. *Color From Rainbows to Lasers*. New York: Thomas Y. Crowell Company, 1978.

Ellinger, Richard G. *Color Structure and Design*. New York: Van Nostrand Reinhold Company, 1980.

Fabri, Ralph. *Color: A Complete Guide for Artists*. New York: Watson-Guptill Publications, 1967.

Gerritsen, Frans. *Theory and Practice of Color*. New York: Van Nostrand Reinhold Company, 1975.

Itten, Johannes. *The Elements of Color*. ed. by Faber Birren. New York: Van Nostrand Reinhard Company, 1970.

McKelvey, Susan. *Light & Shadows*. Lafayette, CA: C & T Publishing, 1989.

Mellor, Susan, and Joost Llffers. *Textile Designs*. New York: Henry N. Abrams, Inc. Publishers, 1991.

Munsell, A. H. *A Color Notation*. Baltimore: Munsell Color Company, Inc., 1946.

Salemme, Lucia A. *Color for the Painter*. New York: Watson-Guptill Publications, 1970.

Yates, Marypaul. *Textiles*. New York: Prentice Hall, 1986.

◆ About the Author ◆

Susan McKelvey is a quilt artist, teacher, and the author of several books on quilting. Her first book, *Color for Quilters*, was published in 1984 and was followed by *Light & Shadows*, which expanded on how color creates the illusion of depth. As she added an interest in writing on quilts to her expertise on color, *Friendship's Offering, Scrolls & Banners to Trace,* and *A Treasury of Quilt Labels* were added. *Color for Quilters II* is a revision of her first book.

Susan has been quilting since 1977, and her work has appeared in museums, galleries, and quilt shows throughout the United States, as well as in magazines and books. She began her own company, Wallflower Designs, in 1987 to design and produce unusual quilt supplies and patterns.

In the days before quilting, Susan earned her B.A. degree in English and Drama at Cornell College and her M.A. in English and Education at the University of Chicago.